Mindsense

Mindsense

A Strengths-Based Approach to Becoming Your Best Self

Dr. Michael J. Provitera

BEP

BUSINESS EXPERT PRESS

Leader in applied, concise business books

Mindsense: A Strengths-Based Approach to Becoming Your Best Self

Cover design by Charlene Kronstedt

Interior design by S4Carlisle Publishing Services, Chennai, India

First published in 2025 by
Business Expert Press, LLC
222 East 46th Street, New York, NY 10017
www.businessexpertpress.com

ISBN-13: 978-1-63742-860-3 (paperback)
ISBN-13: 978-1-63742-861-0 (e-book)

Business Career Development Collection

First edition: 2025

10 9 8 7 6 5 4 3 2 1

EU SAFETY REPRESENTATIVE
Mare Nostrum Group B.V.
Mauritskade 21D
1091 GC Amsterdam
The Netherlands
gpsr@mare-nostrum.co.uk

Description

People that lead their life the fullest share a common secret: They find and develop their strengths to become their best self.

MINDSENSE: A Strengths-Based Approach to Becoming Your Best Self is not your typical self-help book. Its 13 chapters provide practical applications of spotting and developing your strengths. Unlocking your potential and preparing you for a journey of enlightenment.

Dr. Mike shares his unique knowledge of positive psychology to help you reprogram your mind to live your life inside-out as opposed to outside-in. At its core, the book focuses on the concept of self-awareness and knowing thyself. Each chapter includes real-life stories and vignettes that are essential for true enlightenment.

MINDSENSE emphasizes the principle of forgetting things that happened to you in the past and focusing on where you are right now—without worrying about the future. The art of letting go helps you to detach from the crutches that hold you back. This is not a one-time destination but a continuous, engaging process that people that are enlightened commit to. This understanding is crucial to personal well-being and an enlightened life, and *MINDSENSE* will guide you in staying engaged and committed to the process of enlightenment.

MINDSENSE: A Strengths-Based Approach to Becoming Your Best Self promises:

- To help you stop overthinking.
- To help you stop comparing yourself to others because you are more than enough.
- To build superior focus on acting like you're a millionaire.

Begin your path to greatness today—because the best investment you can make is in improving yourself first before attempting to improve others. Your enlightenment journey starts now!

Contents

Preface

Defining MINDSENSE: Mindsense is a group of ideas and concepts orbiting around a core of positive self-regard and being present in the moment.

The irresistible desire to be desired

—Mark Twain

If you are a person that revels in situations, current or past, who keeps rolling the film in your head about situations that take place in your life, and you are frustrated by your lack of control over this, then this book is written for you. You will learn how to use **MINDSENSE**, and you will be "touting about a new feeling of inner peace." This may change the way you think and help you take life day-by-day by living each moment to the fullest.

Think like a millionaire but do not chase wealth. Look at each choice and each quest as the way to cultivate inner wealth. Acting like a millionaire is honoring your own dignity and trusting in your own self-wealth. Abundance flows *through* us not *to* us and it is important to give away our talents with a generous heart. The most valuable asset you have is your mind and growing in self-improvement is a seed for a precious future. Every moment is an irreplaceable resource.

Embrace risk not recklessly but courageously and look at failure as a testing point not a stopping point. Every failure is a TPOV (Teaching Point of View). Noel Tichy, an American management consultant, calls the *Teaching Point of View* a simple concept that all people should have. The Teaching Point of View is how you develop emotional energy and how you motivate yourself to communicate your "best self." Using the TPOV is where you develop your values and ideas on how to improve your life. The TPOV will help you stand in confidence because you trust yourself and you are more authentic.

Trust your time, invest in your growth, and embrace risk as the fire that forges your potential. Cultivate a mindset that gathers abundance and not accumulation because there is inner richness in thinking and acting like a millionaire.

Be grateful for the things in your life, even the trivial things that surround you each day. Try not to get so stressed out about what you cannot control. Control is your enemy; it will always elude you if that is your only focus.

We must be able to sit with ourselves and try to be genuinely happy with self-sufficiency instead of relying on someone else to make us happy. Just be love and love will attract you. Watch what happens. It is simple. The whole idea of self-improvement is a hoax. Begin where you are and be grateful for what you have already accomplished. You will begin to find out that the remarkable things that you do are really happening in the moments of your life. Alan Watts, a philosophical guru, on improving yourself, says that step one is to have the technical ability to accept what happens, and second, you must get out of your own way of your own success.

A Review of *The Power of Now* by Eckhart Tolle

Primarily, I must give Eckhart Tolle a strong positive review. Eckhart is a kind gentle man that is easy to love and very likeable. If you want to learn manifestation, he is one to turn to. He also is big on spirituality. Thus, he incorporates the Lord (primarily Jesus Christ) into his writings and lectures. One thing he says is that when you pray to Jesus, pray with the intention of already having what you pray for. He does not say that Jesus is indicating that you will get it but that you already have it because you asked. Tolle feels that Jesus automatically gives you what you want within reason. Alan Watts said it perfectly about how religion works in mindsense:

Watts says that it is our thinking that is causing us all the trouble. Liberate yourself from the perpetuality uncalculated life in the present. Jesus said, on the sermon of the mount, "My followers, be not anxious about tomorrow, the uncalculated

life that unfolds tomorrow awaits you. If my father was so righteous to clothe the grass and the field, do you feel that he will not clothe you with much more, do not be so faithless about tomorrow."

This is one of the few times that I mention spirituality and religion in *Mindsense* because this book is not geared toward this type of spiritual approach. Mentioned here once, and there is nothing wrong with spirituality and religion in self-help books. Spirituality is important and this book focuses on the power of the universe. It is the universe that will manifest things into your life. Therefore, for more on spirituality, see Eckhart's work on *The Power of Now*.

Vignette—The Possible Truth About The Power of Now

As Alan Watts pointed out in his writings "Embracing the Present Moment," the present is all that matters. Watts argues that time is a measure of motion and that we do not see what our life consists in each moment. When a cat comes along, the head comes first and the tail follows; it is all one cat, and the whole cat moves. The same with us, our life goes together. Watts states that if you want to define yourself as a billiard ball, then you will play life like the past was responsible for your present moment, and if you believe it hard enough, you will feel it, and what happened to practically all of us is the result of who we are in the moment. So, we do not realize that we are living out the now and throwing the past behind us. Watts argues that who you think you are is highly dependent on the people that told you who you are, but you are not that person that people tell you are. You are who you tell yourself you are. In his book titled *Zen*, Watts puts it simply:

Yet however much we may try to delay or grasp the moment, the fact remains that while, from one point of view, it eludes us, from another, we cannot get away from it. We may try to lag behind in the past or to hurry on into the future, but inevitably we do our lagging or hurrying in the present moment. As soon as we realize that the current moment is, in reality, inescapable, we shall no longer try to grasp it; for whether we know it or not, it grasps us. The now, this present moment, is reality. All things proceed from it and exist in it.

On occasion, time is bothersome to people. Most people say that they have no time. Alan Watts argues that because people are not aware of the present moment that they are in right now, they lose track of time. The present is just a spotlight for people instead of a head light. Stay in the spotlight and enjoy the moment.

Tolle states in his book titled *The Power of Now*, which made him famous, that the present is the only real time we have. Watts founded this point because in the present moment, there is no past and there is no future, and there never will be.

We imagine ourselves to be results of the past. We do not realize that the past is caused by the present moment at the time it happened. He expresses our past as the ship's wake. The wake of ship flows back from the prow. The wake does not drive the ship any more than the tail wags the dog.

Many of us have excuses for where we are in the present moment. The truth of the matter is that your present moment all begins here right now with you. You determine your moment and nothing else can impact your moment but you. This is where creation begins.

***

In reality, Eckhart Tolle was a disgruntled person as a child. At 30 years, he lived with his mom. He had no job, no health benefits, no money, no prospects, and just walked out of the Cambridge graduate school in London. Walking out of a prestigious university with nothing to show for is a truly incalculable risk. Undoubtedly, the world looked at him as a failure. He also felt like a failure. One night while sleeping, he woke up to a pounding heartbeat. He said to himself, "I think I should kill myself." At that point, he realized that the mind is separate from himself. He said to himself, "Who is this self that I want to kill?" The next day he woke up with an epiphany. He realized that his mind is separate from himself. He began writing *The Power of Now*. A colossal success.

Tolle was on to something big. It was not that he invented the power of now, his idea is self-explanatory and has been part of humanity since the beginning of time. What Tolle did was he brought the idea to life. He created a commonsense idea for people that thought it was uncommon to focus on the power of now.

Mindsense will focus on the current moment. Living each moment in peace and prosperity. This idea, too, is nothing new. A woman on a dating site, 54, said, "I believe in making every moment count and cherishing the simple joys in life." People are aware of the common sense of the present moment, but many people do not use the current moment to their advantage. My book offers nothing new, but if you read it, you will be more enlightened, better equipped to face the day-to-day struggles in life, and you will be able to have an essence about you that can manifest anything you genuinely want. You will become a magnet and people will love you.

Acknowledgments

To the many people throughout my life that have helped me along my journey. To my mother Ann, my sister Patti, and my father Frank. To my girlfriend Clouie, who is the wind beneath my wings, and her mother Louise, both of them are great business leaders. To my daughters Janet and Lauren. To Sister Mary Fran Fleischaker, Sister Linda Bevilacqua, Sister Peggy Coyne, Sister Carmen Alvarez and all the Adrian Dominican Sisters that inspired me to write this book.

Dr. Joe Hair, my dissertation chair, Dr. Gordon DiPaolo, my first professor, mentor, and friend.

To my children, Janet, and Lauren, who every day inspire me to work hard and do my best at everything I do and everyone I touch.

To my students that I teach and the executives that I train, who I owe every success and every cherished moment of learning and growing with them.

To Jim Clawson, my colleague and friend from Harvard Business School, who has inspired me to teach with passion and train executives with both heart and mind.

To Victor Sino, executive at HSBC, and Jeanty Remy, the first executive that I coached when I began Motivational Leadership Training, thank you both for your friendship and encouragement.

To Scott Isenberg and Charlene Kronstedt, my colleagues in publishing and editing at Business Expert Press, who by being present in my life have taught me the professional publishing business. This book would not be possible without their encouragement.

To Dr. Josh Steiner and Dr. Sam Lerman, MD, Hollywood, Florida. Two of the best doctors in North America that always helped me stay energized and healthy to keep me on track with my livelihood.

To the Center for Positive Organizations at the Stephen M. Ross School of Business at the University of Michigan and Bob Quinn, Jane Dutton, and Gretchen Spreitzer, for their research on the Reflected Best Self Exercise (RBSE) in which I coach and facilitate.

Special thanks to Bob Stocking and Rosalyn Murphy at EnlivenWork for their leadership and support for the RBSE Global Community Coach and Facilitators.

Introduction

There is a greater need for learners to reinvent themselves and acquire new or complementary skills.

—Docprov

Tolle's book, within 3 years, helped him to become famous. His fame may have been due to his luck of getting on *The Oprah Winfrey Show*, and that endorsement certainly helped him a great deal. Publicity is key in the commercial world of selling books. Fortunately for Tolle, he has sold over 12 million copies, and his book is translated into over 21 languages.

If I can help one person become happier and more enlightened, perhaps **YOU**, if you decide to keep reading my book, *Mindsense*, I will be satisfied for the rest of my life!

This critical acclaim of E. Tolle is noteworthy to say the least. However, *The Power of Now*, while being the terrific book that it is, is lacking in some ways. It does speak about the current moment and how to live in the NOW with peace and being fully aware. The drawback to this notion is that while it is absolutely true that we must live in the NOW, we must be realistic in that our moments may be camouflaged by extending thoughts that need to be tempered. For instance, the five general stages of grief, as described by Elisabeth Kübler-Ross, may impact our thinking and discourage living in the NOW. Elisabeth Kübler-Ross, a Harvard University professor, was a Swiss-American psychiatrist, a pioneer in near-death studies, and author of the internationally best-selling book *On Death and Dying*. She first discussed her theory of the five stages of grief, also known as the "Kübler-Ross model." She argues that for everything that happens to us, big or small, minor or major, trivial or debilitating, we must go through a moment-to-moment thought process until it is handled or dealt with. If grief shows its ugly face to us while we are alive, which it almost always does in some way, once the process that Ross touts about is over, we may be able to go back to what Tolle calls the "Power of Now."

The Kübler-Ross model helps us process our current moment coming to us from our mind and through our thoughts. Here is an example of how the Kübler-Ross model may transpire and help you stay in the moment:

Denial: This cannot be happening.

Anger: Why did this happen? Who is to blame?

Bargaining: Try to ensure that this may not happen again.

Depression: Sometimes bargaining is not enough, and some people cannot bear the situation; I am too sad to do anything.

Acceptance: You acknowledge that this has happened, and you cannot change it. You cannot go back in time. It is what it is. You must go on. Upon acceptance, you begin to stay in the current moment and not let this bother you any longer. You are a stronger person.

For the moments that follow, the five stages of grief may appear to be steps in the thought process, but they are not. They are a cycle of recovery that we all need to go through in life at some point in time. Kübler-Ross said that the mental thought processing is as individual as our fingerprints are and is not a linear process that can be handled in a moment, in a few minutes, in a day, or even in a week. It must run its course in both our thoughts and in our minds. We should talk about it with our loved ones or our friends, however. Talking it through provides a way to pass through the process and it helps us put the episode behind us. Once it is behind us, we can return to living in the moment with acceptance, gratitude, and resilience. This makes "Mindsense."

The greatest obstacle that we face is our ego. In your consciousness, you can create a life that realizes that the ego, in practice, is a sense of strain. When you think about yourself, you are dealing with the ego. When you think of your entire world or the universe in which you live, your ego weakens, and you live a better life in enlightenment.

When you miss a step or cannot reach a certain level, the ego revels in this diminished goal—leaving you with only your mind and thoughts to contend with. Mindsense helps people refocus and branch out where they are instead of being so hard on themselves. Overthinking is a real problem. In many cases, our problems are short term, but our ego attempts to make them linger longer than necessary.

Sigmund Freud pointed out that there is a psychology of *accident-prone individuals*—a state in which drivers attract their own problems. There are people that go around looking for accidents and this may be consciously and, in many ways, unconsciously. They seem to be attracting trouble like light attracts moths.

In the long term, our awareness is the essence of our self-leadership and the way to master mindsense. There was a terrific book written about this titled *Leadership and Self-Deception*, which is still a big seller by Berrett-Koehler Publishers, with over two million copies sold. The Arbinger Institute states that the key to self-leadership is not in what we do but in who we are and what we blind ourselves from. We, on occasion, unwittingly sabotage the effectiveness of our own efforts to achieve happiness. Thus, when we consistently tap into and act on our own innate sense of what is right for us, we can dramatically improve our lives. Overthinking is the cause of many of our problems. This self-deception can be controlled with "Mindsense."

True addiction, like cigarettes or other vices are just lurking about and easy to grasp. The problem is that we sometimes have to try to not think of what we do not want, because at some instance, we are our own worst enemy. Earl Nightingale had it right when he published his work on "Think and Grow Rich." Earl had it right with this great idea.

Unfortunately, our enemy and our ally are our own ego. It is an interesting concept that if we master our own freedom from our own ego, we can be free from ourselves and our own torment from our ego. Letting our ego get the best of us is similar to the methadone program offered to heroin addicts in the 1970s and 1980s. The program attempted to get drug addicts off heroin to introduce a new drug that is less potent. The methadone program solved one problem while opening up another one. However, that shift in thinking was somewhat helpful for heroin addicts. The same thing may happen with you. Using mindsense, if you replace your overthinking with relaxation and mindfulness, you begin to be still, accepting, and awakening as a person of substance, then you begin to become more attractive to others and people want to be around you.

Another interesting concept that is used often is affirmations. Positive affirmations promised a change for the better by having your mind go over and over the things you want to feel, the things that you want to manifest, and the things that you do not currently have but want.

Mindsense uses a suggestion that you create your own affirmations for where you are right now and where you would like to be in the future.

Clement Stone, an American businessperson, and self-help book author said set up a daily mantra for positive self-suggestion. Use auto suggestion and tell yourself that you are on track and doing well. Just saying "I am good," and "I am OK" is immensely powerful.

This way of thinking helps direct your intentions in the moment and attempts to change the way you feel about yourself. Ensure that you read your affirmation in the morning and night and perhaps throughout the day. The best affirmations come from Alan Watts. Here is his expert opinion of the nine affirmations to say to yourself before you begin your day as you whisper a few truths to yourself every morning. Imagine the kind of days you will have and the peace of mind that you will carry with you throughout the day.

1. I am open to change; I do not resist the unknown.
2. I will be present to listen to life's symphony and to savior this moment here in this very instant that we truly exist.
3. I am whole and I do not look for flaws to fix and I practice self-acceptance.
4. I release my grip, and I surrender real power and trust the universe that guides me, and my path is my own.
5. I trust my journey each step as part of a grand unfolding.
6. I choose kindness and I nurture gentleness within my heart with everyone I meet.
7. I cherish the simple things such as silence, dawn, and sunset and I do not overlook life's beauty.
8. I am grateful for all the joys and sorrows, and I have gratitude.
9. I will treat myself with tenderness and remember to promise myself that I will be easy on myself.

Upon waking each morning, use mindsense to start out by listening to the voice inside your mind. Will it build you up or tear you down.

We have the power to change the message that we are telling ourselves. At first, try it for the next 5 days, then try it for the next 21 days. It takes 21 days to break a habit or create a new habit. However, recent research indicates that the 21 days to break a habit may actually be 18 to 254 depending on the person and the habit so take your time and be patient as you attempt to change a habit or create a new one. In Lally's study, titled "How Are Habits Formed in the Real World," published in the *European Journal of Social Psychology* in 2018, it took anywhere from 18 to 254 days for people to break a habit or to form a new one. This study has not been replicated, however, and only included 39 participants. Use the 21-day rule as your optimum test but be aware that habit breaking, and habit forming is a process that takes time.

The notion is that a habit can be broken or formed in 21 days with consistent effort was first coined by:

Dr. Maxwell Maltz, a plastic surgeon who wrote the book "Psycho-Cybernetics" in 1960; he observed that his patients took around 21 days to adjust to their new appearance after surgery, which he then applied to the concept of habit formation, though research now shows this timeframe is not accurate for everyone and can vary significantly depending on the habit and individual. (Found on Public Domain)

As it turns out, our mind can become a constant think tank that reminds us of what we do not have and what we want but cannot get, and therefore the 21-day habit formation is an approximation. Worthy of your knowledge and implementation.

Speak to yourself not as a critic but as an evaluator of positive living. Acknowledge negative thoughts and do not try to suppress them. Use self-talk saying this to yourself:

I am here now and that is all that matters. I am healthy, I am alive and free.

Begin your day with an awareness and observe your thoughts in the moment. Speak to yourself, "*I am enough right here right now!*" Do not strive to push too hard on yourself, be understanding, if you feel fear, it is all right to be afraid, if you feel lost, say to yourself, even in the mist of this chaos, "*I am on the path to righteousness.*"

Earl Nightingale felt that if you change the way your think, you can manifest wonderful things. This is profound. Just act on and in the moment, catch yourself, accept it and move on. This will help you temper your ego and be happier where you are and where you are going. Manifesting does work and we want to feel and think of what we want to become in the future and let the universe be our guide. Visualization works but it must be followed up with action in the form of behavior to secure your accomplishments.

Your mind must be your ally. A thought comes into your mind, you must decide if you want to accept or dwell on it or not. You cannot control your thoughts, but you can control whether you accept them or not. Do not be hard on yourself because a thought surfaced. The mind is so powerful that thoughts just appear for no reason and accepting the thought or simply moving on from it is the best way to handle it.

During COVID-19, the mind was continually active in the middle of the night. Eventually, most of us realized that there is nothing we can do but get up, live with our feelings of restlessness until we get tired again. This was hard for people that needed to get up to work and take care of children, dogs, and other family members. Thus, the stress became a circular problem. Lack of sleep, wondering mind, restlessness, and the same cycle repeats. COVID-19 is over now, and some residual effects may still be traced in our daily habits. The key is to reinvent yourself to adjust to what is in the present moment and face reality as it is and not how you wish it to be.

When you can picture yourself in your favorite place, the beach, the mountains, at sea, or in the woods, you begin to realize that nothing truly matters but the surroundings in which you find yourself, the people that you are with, and those that love you—either close by or from afar. Past or present, they still may have impacted your life in some way. Plant positive seeds in your mind and then watch your life transform like a beautiful garden with the right amount of sun and water. ENGAGE YOURSELF IN *mindsense* AND LESS NONSENSE

CHAPTER 1

Your Moment Is Your Friend

A Winner is a dreamer that never gave up.

—Nelson Mandela

What a man or woman can be, he or she must be.

—Abraham Maslow

The most important obstacle to an enlightened life is a mind that continues to sabotage your current moment with thoughts of the past and concerns for the future. If you look at your head as a football, American football that is, your mind, as a football, would get a touchdown evert time. Your mind is not a football and the problem with your mind is that it is so elusive that it is not easy to control. Getting a touchdown, therefore, is to let your mind react whichever way it wants to and then manage the thoughts that are processed by your mind. The football is up, and you can catch it or deflect it; that is your thought-provoking mechanism. We do not know why we have so many of the same thoughts reoccurring, but it could drive you to become worrisome or you can deal with the thoughts as they enter your mind, knowing that this too shall pass. The key here is to catch yourself and laugh without being so judgmental of yourself. You do something wrong, you say that is not like me. You do something right, you say that is like me; I always do things right. Self-talk is key to your success and keeping your thoughts at bay.

Vignette—The Frog and the Scorpion

A frog was once sitting by the edge of a vast lake. A scorpion joins the frog at the edge of the water and places himself next to the frog. The frog looks over and wonders what a scorpion would want with him.

The scorpion notices the frog looking over the water and says: "Hello, my friend, I see you are about to jump in the river and swim to the other side."

The frog says, "That is correct but what's that got to do with you?"

The scorpion says,

Well my friend, I need to get to other side to join my family, but I cannot swim. So, would you be kind enough to let me hop on your back and you deposit me on the other side of the lake?

The frog looks perplexed and says, "Oh no, I know you scorpions, you sting frogs and kill them. We would get out there on the lake and you would sting me, and I would drown and die. So, forget about that, FRIEND!" The frog says loudly and in the scorpion's face.

The scorpion replies, "Wait a minute, with your little frog brain you are not thinking. If I were to sting you, you would drown and die, and so would I because I cannot swim."

The frog thinks this logic over and says, "OK, hop on." They embark into the lake.

The frog and the scorpion hit midpoint, and the scorpion stings the frog. The frog and the scorpion go down and come back up as the venom from the scorpion singes the frog to say one last comment. "Why, why, why would you do this, I am about to drown and die and so are you, why would you do that."

The scorpion yells as loud as possible right before they both drown: "Because I am a scorpion, and it is my nature as a scorpion to sting frogs and kill them."

The frog takes his last breath before drowning, the scorpion also loses his breath, and they both drown at the same time.

***

The moral of the story is do not carry a scorpion on your back.

Your mind is the scorpion, at times, and your mind can act like the scorpion. The nature of the mind is regulated by the ego. The ego wants you to be safe by encouraging you to know your limitations. The ego does not like to be made a fool of, so it will keep you in your comfort zone and give you excuses to limit your success, to limit your enlightenment, and to limit your manifestation.

Buddhists believe that it is possible to end a life of suffering, psycho-logical suffering that is, and ascertain a life of enlightenment through meditating, growing, and learning, in order to have inner peace.

My mother always told me that she wanted peace of mind. She had lots of stress in her life, and she wanted to relax in the moment and not worry any more. I wanted her to have that too, and I tried to help her as much as I could. I bought her a dishwasher when washing dishes by hand were the norm. But I failed as a little boy. I could only do so much at the age of 13.

My father went through a midlife crisis, and he strayed on her with another woman. She cried in her room at night, and I went to comfort her. I asked her what was wrong as she stared into her mirror or at the edge of her bed.

"Mom, what's wrong?" I asked.

"Oh Michael, please go, I am so sad, I am sorry."

"Why mom, why, what's wrong?" I asked inquisitively.

"Your father is having an affair," she said weeping.

"An affair?" I asked. I was 13 years old, and I had no clue what she was talking about, but then I realized that I had experienced an event related to what she was talking about. I remembered one time when he left me in a car alone and I was scared and frightened while he visited someone for an hour or so in an apartment. Children were not supposed to be left in a car alone and I was very scared.

At a very young age, I watched my dad with another woman and was left in the car all alone.

At my mom's bedside, I tried to console her. As I was just a young boy at 13, there was no way I could stop her from crying. She would cry in a voice that could knock the socks off a young boy.

"What did I do, what did I do to deserve this?" She said, in a singing voice, these words as a question that she did not want answered.

It was a wailing tone that I will never forget.

She did nothing to cause this affair; she was an angel. Everybody knew she was a great woman and obviously my dad did too until he went through his midlife crisis.

I failed as a young boy. Yet that failure made me resilient, made me stronger, and with resilience, I was able to take on much bigger challenges in my life. As bad as failure is, it echoes throughout your life with lessons that prepare you for life's struggles and challenges.

In Benjamin Hall's book titled *Resolute,* he feels that resilience is the key to success in life. Through all his interviews with people that have been severely afflicted by wars and other tragedies, he found that they have the wherewithal inside of them to bounce back with resilience. Ben feels that resilience should be taught in school for youngsters.

Later in life as my mom got older, I noticed that she read romance novels continuously, four of five at a time. She had them stacked up beside her bed. She read before sleep. Perhaps to read about a life that she wished she had. I do not know for sure what compelled her to read so much.

Mindsense is good to know but there is no guarantee that it will stop the thoughts that influence our life because I am sure she could forgive my father, but she could never forget what he did to her.

Once you break someone's spirit in love, there almost is no true recovery. I certainly could never fully forgive him or forget his affair either. One time, I was saying something negative about my father to my uncle Michael. Uncle Mike said, "Never disrespect your father." Uncle Mike was my father's godfather, and I was named after him. From that time on, I never disrespected my father again. In fact, I, often to this day, praise my father.

I act out the good things he did and bury the bad—escalating the jovialness and warm heart he had for children and adults while not imitating his trait of infidelity and gambling.

We learn good things from our parents, and if we can, we bury the skeletons in the closet.

My father was a brilliant man and great football player. Upon graduating high school, scouts selected him for Ivy League colleges, such as Dartmouth, and Champlain College along with many other universities who wanted to enroll him so that he could play quarterback for their football team. Unfortunately, he was drafted into WWII and watched Germany crumble before his own eyes.

Upon returning from war, my dad just wanted to get married and settle down.

Sometimes, it takes Mindsense to live with your thoughts and survive, and we attempt to do the best we can with the people we love to help weed out the negative thought patterns that occasionally resurface.

There is also another side that is daunting; people that may hear a story like this may knock you or feel that the apple does not fall far from the tree. Disregard that nonsense.

At the time, I did not understand why I could not reach my mom and help her to stop crying. What capacity could a young boy have to help an adult stop crying? We all must know our limitations and not be so hard on ourselves. Learn to be kinder to yourself.

She would say things that can reverberate in my mind.

"Oh, Michael, you're a young boy, you would not understand," as she continued crying in my arms.

I would watch and hear her wailing by my side as she began withering down in weight to 98 pounds as she felt so distraught. I knew that the thoughts in her mind were much more powerful than my condolence and sympathy for her.

I felt as if there was nothing I can do but stay by her side as she wept.

When my sister Patti would surface after hearing her mom crying, she would ask a question to me.

"What is wrong, Michael, why is mom crying?" with a caring tone of a 9-year-old and a kind heart wanting to help, tears in her eyes with an inquisitive stare at the room where her mom was crying.

"Sorry Patti, mom's sad right now, there is nothing you can do, please go to bed, and I will take care of it for us," I would say convincingly without a doubt that I knew that I was not being honest with her. Patti would go back to her room sad, and I would try to console her.

There was literally nothing that I can do to help my mom and being there by her side may have made it worse because she may have felt more embarrassed that she could not control her sadness in front of her little boy.

While it was daunting for me as a young boy, I never forget how terrible it was for her. Her present moments were torrid for a long time. I survived that trauma and so did my mom.

Things were so bad that her boss, at Wagner College, where she worked as an office manager for 35 years, asked her to leave dad. He watched her become frail, sad, and heartbroken. He wanted to give my mom a better life and part of me agreed with him. She deserved better. My mom was not going to leave my dad, and she turned her boss's proposal down.

My father eventually came back to her, and the family stayed intact until she died.

She was never the same again, however. Her sad thoughts impacted her life, and the sorrow was shadowed by the mind recalling her past in the present moment.

On her death stone, my sister Patti had something written that represented her life, probably building on the Christmas movie with a similar title but just as well.

"She Was A Wonderful Life."

Her godson is the famous American ice hockey player Nick Fotiu, who played in the World Hockey Association and National Hockey League between 1974 and 1988. Nick showed up at her funeral burial plot, at the time of burial, with two live pure white doves. He opened the cage. One flew away free, while the other flew to a tree nearby.

When the priest said the famous last words for Ann, my mother, that she is on her way now to heaven, a few leaves moved at the top of a tree as her soul passed on the way to heaven.

With the vast opportunity upon us, why settle for less than a life of inner peace. You should enjoy every moment of your existence while you are breathing with life's abundance all around you.

My father would tell me, build a house son, have a family with a white picket fence. This is great advice but, in some ways, limiting. With Mindsense, you can have it all: *Money, Fame, Love, Family, Significant Other, Partner, Car, Boat, Home, and Great Relationships.* You can have everything you want; all you have to do is go out and get it. Manifest it in your mind and thoughts and suspend your ego that holds you back from your achievements.

Remember that you are not alone, and you are very much loved. Loved by your siblings even if they do not call, loved by your children and grandchildren even if they only see you on holidays, the fact is that people send you positive thoughts daily and through synchronicity, you pick them up. Your ears ring and thoughts enter your mind from someone that you care about. This is because you are living in the moment.

Wayne Dyer says that "When you change the way you look at something, what you work at, changes for the better." Everything begins to change around you in a good way.

Earl Nightingale called it attitude shift, and he said that "ATTITUDE" is the magic word in his book *Think and Grow Rich*.

The magic word in this book is "GRATITUDE."

You must learn to free yourself from your mind. You have a joker voice inside you that is like a villain, a critic, and an opponent. It holds you back from becoming who you were truly meant to be. We often find ourselves commenting on our shortfalls to ourselves. We keep running the tape on the worst things that ever happened to us in our mind. We lose something; we feel like a failure.

Our voice in our mind speculates why we ended up a certain way, why things are not going so great for us, and how bad things could get in the future. You judge what someone has over you and compare yourself to everyone that has slightly more than you. People we don't know but hear about or see sets up a picture in our mind as happier and more content than us. Free yourself of comparison.

If you cast a doubt on your livelihood and let that be your mantra you will only see the impossible.

If you step into the future with certainty and with a heart and mind full of trust in yourself, you build an abundant life. The future flows freer of doubt and despair and your setbacks dissipate. You radiate trust and security.

With each setback and loss, you rise up with talents that you never even knew you had, and you become more resilient. Whatever happens in your life you rise to the occasion.

The way you perceive the world is the way the world views you. If you expect to have problems with work, relationships, health, or anything else, it finds its way to appear in your life but if you expect things to flow smoothly, they usually do. Imagine if you expect things not to work out and they do.

Why waste your energy on unnecessary stress, worrying about things that, most likely, will never happen.

With Mindsense, the moment is where you conduct your life and plan and appreciate the people and circumstances that you find yourself in. Never doubt your existence. You are doing great!

Life is not a dress rehearsal. We only have the moments that we live each day. The someday and the wait for happiness are far away and may be missed if we do not live in the moment and spend time enjoying each moment.

The present is where every moment becomes meaningful. Ask yourself, "Am I awake?" Embrace who you are without fear.

Do not reach the end of your life living your life based on someone else's script.

Time moves with a relentless rhythm. We push things to tomorrow, but time is ours to command. Time is intangible and searching for tomorrow does not truly exist until we get there. Eckhart Tolle recalls a bar in London with a sign that says, "Free Beer Tomorrow." You are always seeking, chasing something out of reach that you expect to come in the future.

When we truly stop to reflect, we realize that we must awaken and live each day as a true opportunity to appreciate and to be engaged and to be fully present in every moment.

Judging in most cases could actually be accurate.

Daniel Kahneman, a Nobel Prize winner in economics, author of *Thinking, Fast and Slow*, stated that judging things are more accurate than chance guessing would be, and, therefore, it is OK to judge things. Here are a few examples that impact the way we judge things:

- On most occasions, people who act friendly are in fact friendly.
- A professional athlete who is very tall and thin is much likely to play basketball than football.
- People with a PhD are more likely to subscribe to *The New York Times* than people who ended their education after high school.
- Young men are more likely than elderly women to drive aggressively.

In all these cases and in many others, there is some truth to the stereotypes that govern our judgments or the predictions that follow.

The mind looks at what we like and wishes it had more of it. Wayne Dyer said, "We can never get enough of what we don't want." That ice cream in the refrigerator is calling you; those cookies, in the cookie jar, are hard to turn down. The mind focuses on our dislikes and places them on the forefront of our thoughts. This is overthinking, and takes away from living in the moment.

The voice in our mind is not necessarily relevant to the situation while all this overthinking is carrying on. I had a great doctor, Dr. Weintraub, on Madison Avenue in Manhattan, New York, that once told me that "You are healthy until proven different." He said this because I thought I had an upper respiratory problem or some other ailment. He was reassuring me that I am OK. Thus, you must rise above these thoughts that are bringing you down and realize that it is your mind that is keeping you complacent and focusing on the wrong things. You have to start your day happy and content.

"You are great until proven different." That is right; you are great at everything you put your mind to. Thinking of the glass half full gives you the impetus to change your mind to help you achieve what you want to accomplish, and if you do this, there is a strong chance that you will be great at what you want to become or create in yourself, your business, and your life. The mind is powerful, and you can control it.

You have to change the neuroplasticity of your brain, rewire it with positive thoughts.

Stop nurturing old wounds. Catch your mind before you lose it. Say to yourself, "Here I go again, rehearsing my past and attempting to predict my future." Then laugh out loud to yourself.

You began in this world with DNA, which is your program. Then, as a younger person, you learned many things from your parents, uncles, aunts, grandparents, teachers, and society. Your success platform is found inside your mind and has been programmed since you were very young.

My program told me that I cannot help my mother, and I am a failure. I had to reprogram that feeling of not being able to console a grown woman, my mom, and make her feel better, or I would have never had a relationship with a woman when I grew up.

If we tap into our newly discovered programs that override the old ones from our childhood, we can succeed at just about anything.

If we keep doing what we have always done, we may only become mediocre in life or we may never find our true passion. Your true north is not on a roadmap, you must go out and find it. Becoming a success is a habitual act that you have to focus on as much as possible. As you develop this awareness, you either see positiveness in yourself or you see lack. If you see lack, you have to reprogram that thought process. Have gratitude for what you have.

Your thinking is like your thermostat, you turn it down and the air gets cooler, turn it up and the cooling of the air stops. The same with your mind. If you set the right temperature in your mind, then you live for that moment with the right thoughts and a peace of mind.

Goal setting is also an important attribute of success. John F. Kennedy set a goal to have astronauts go to the moon.

On May 25, 1961, President John F. Kennedy announced before a special joint session of Congress the dramatic and ambitious goal of sending an American safely to the Moon before the end of the decade.

President Kennedy manifested his goal and so could you.

"We choose to go to the moon in this decade and do the other things, not because they are easy, but because they are hard," Kennedy told the crowd at Rice University in Houston. The president promised to put a man on the moon before the end of the decade, and seven years later, he delivered, with the Apollo 11 moon landing in 1969.

People do not resist change; they resist being changed. It makes mindsense to discover your best goals in the moment and plan them in that moment, and then watch them manifest.

Reaching enlightenment is about rising above the mantra of thoughts that your mind continues to pervade you. The brain is an important organ and the thoughts that it creates are instrumental on how you feel. How you react to certain situations, and how you expect others to react to you is important.

Maslow once argued that if the only tool you have in your toolbox is a hammer, then everything looks like a nail.

If you lack the tools to tame the mind and the thoughts that it produces, you are doomed to become enlightened.

You must call on your mind when you need it and at other times, just leave it be. Relax your mind, comfort it, and give it the protein it needs to survive.

When I work with children and train them on future career success in KAPOW (Kids and the Power of Work), in Miami, Florida, I often noticed that when I ask them a question or to come up in front of the class, I see them all wanting to role play and present. Children that are reserved and shy sometimes lack the protein to think. When we would be at a lunch presentation, I would see what the shy and withdrawn student had for lunch. They had potato chips, soda, and desert. I realized then that the fuel we put in our body provides us with the stimulus we receive. Fast food equals fast thoughts, while healthy food equals controlled, calm, cool, and focused thoughts.

When you have a task that you need to complete, you sit down and focus by calling on your mind and your thoughts. Now your mind is being used for the current moment while preparing for the future moment in which, when it occurs, you will then be there at that current moment.

Once you accomplish something that you have manifested, you rest, you rejuvenate, you go on vacation, and, most importantly, you celebrate by rewarding yourself.

When your mind creates a leakage of vital energy, feed it protein, and relax it until you must call upon it again. It's OK, you will be OK, do not worry. Any intense relationship will have residual thought influx until it dissipates. For some people, the compulsive thoughts are good for them because that is all that they have left. A widow with memories stays active and somewhat healthy by keeping things the same for as long as possible. The loss is less debilitating and more manageable with the artifacts and memories. However, at some point, the widow must let go.

Being addicted to someone, however, means that you no longer have the control to stop it. The more you let yourself identify with your thinking, it becomes you, recalls what you liked, and perhaps what you disliked. You are overthinking the past situation that no longer exists. You are punishing yourself for no reason. You did nothing wrong; relationships do not always work, people are different. Life happens, relationships end on occasion, and other doors open, better things could happen as long as you are open to going into the new. You will survive and you will be OK. You are OK.

To be conscious of your present moment or situation, relax the judgments and interpretations of yourself. Be kind to yourself. If you are letting your mind run amok, you cannot stop it, and you are staying in what is called unconscious despair. If you let this happen, it will not grow, and you will not be enlightened.

Earl Nightingale created "The Strangest Secret," and he spoke about a farmer planting parsley and nightshade. Nightshade is poison. The farmer watered both of the seeds in their own location on the farm, and they both grew with the same sun and water. This is the same with the seeds that you plant in your mind. Your thoughts, if you let them control you and you keep watering them and giving them sunshine, they will grow no matter if you want them to grow or not.

This also happens in your subconscious, if you keep thinking about a past scenario, it is stored in your subconscious and will filter into your current thoughts. To prosper, think positive thoughts.

If you keep thinking of the past, you are watching consciousness grow, the stronger the emotional energy charge will be for that past occurrence, the more it will be debilitating to your growth and development.

The key is to feel the emotion, feel the hurt, feel the loneliness, feel bad if you have to, feel lonely, feel abandoned, and sit with that feeling until it passes.

Nourish positive thoughts to replace those negative feelings and thoughts and that will rewire your brain. Rewiring the brain is the process of changing the brain's neural pathways through new experiences, new practices, and with new consistency.

This process is called Neuroplasticity

Festering sad thoughts and feeling a sense of loneliness is nurturing and keeping the thoughts alive. Leaving the thoughts behind or at least, at first, acknowledging that they exist is the first step to enlightenment.

Unfortunately, you cannot control your thoughts. The stronger and the longer the relationship, the longer the thoughts of loss will linger. It is OK, you will be OK. Time heals all wounds.

The thoughts will eventually dissipate even if you have not found a new partner, or new job, or new life situation. Feeling underwhelmed with a lack of energy and will power, may lead to negative emotions and behavior that can lead to ulcers, high blood pressure, or migraines. Just like watching a sunset lowers blood pressure, thinking of a past relationship raises blood pressure.

The enlightened life is composed of the emotions and behavior that you manifest in yourself every day. Be aware of your emotions and attempt to control your behavior. Try to do this with intention. Wayne Dyer in his book titled *The Power of Intention*, provides great advice.

> *Intention is generally viewed as a certain kind of determination propelling one to succeed at all costs by never giving up on an inner picture. He explores intention as something you do, as an energy you're a part of. He looks at intention as a field of energy that you can access to begin co-creating your life with the power of intention.*—Wayne Dyer

From now on, when you are about to do something, start by saying to yourself, "I intend to do this." This will bring harmony to both your thoughts and your intention.

Harmony is constructive when you have gratitude and kindness in your heart. Emotion is the body's reaction to your thoughts in your mind. Unconscious mental emotional reactive patterns bond together when the body and mind feels a certain emotion due to your thoughts. Catch yourself feeding your emotions with thoughts that are positive. Control your behavior and fuel your life with exercise, nature, pets, and companionship.

Quantum physics offers an amazing science to help you evolve.

- Principle number one is that consciousness is creating our life experiences. Control your consciousness by changing your own consciousness and you can change your world.
- Principle number two is to use your emotions that are fed from your thoughts in your mind as signals to realize that you may be on or off track a bit. Then get right back on being positive, gracious, and kind to yourself and others.

Sometimes we keep doing the same thing and results do not appear. Persistence without a plan may not help you manifest what you want. Plan well and be persistent. Follow through on your goals.

Vignette—Flies Never Win

The key in life is working smarter, not harder. People may be trying too hard doing the same things over and over again and getting the same result.

This is a story about garlic salt and the persistent fly.

People try too hard and feel that they need to have consistent effort. Effort is important and so is consistency, but this effort and consistency must be performed correctly so that success happens.

Same as in sports. Working hard consistently works but if you are not doing well on the field, it may be because of your lacking the correct effort and consistency in the gym. Ergo, your exercise routine may be weak.

It was a warm day in Florida, and I am listening to a young girl scream out in my kitchen.

My daughter Lauren screamed out loud.

"Dad, there is a small fly burning out its life in a last-ditch effort to get out of the garlic salt container," she exclaimed.

The top of the container was open, and the holes were not covered. The fly crawled into a hole on top of the garlic saltshaker attempting to eat.

The top of the container was left open by accident and the shaker holes were exposed. The fly entered the garlic saltshaker.

Now, as my daughter is screaming my name, the fly is making futile attempts to get out. The several attempts to escape caused the fly to simply try harder. The persistent effort of the fly did not set him free.

The fly just kept pushing up and banging off the top, missing the exit holes each time, not knowing that if he just took his time, and figured out how to exit, he would be set free. The fly is pounding at the top of the opened garlic salt container but not heading toward the small holes at the top. The exact hole that he entered freely.

The fly has a frenzied effort that offers no hope for survival. The fly is trapped by its own way of thinking because it cannot find the hole in which it got in. The fly is doomed to die trying.

With only a fraction of the effort wasted, the fly can just find the hole to freedom.

The fly does not find the hole and will die after bouncing off the top of the shaker even though the holes are open and would make it easy to allow for a safe exit.

The same idea can relate to human beings. We just keep trying to break through barriers by doing the same thing over and over again and we hope for a different outcome. We grind it out and hustle harder. If we just looked at our strategy, we could simply change. The fly would crawl out of the hole if it knew how.

The moral of the story is that people can change, and obviously, flies cannot. Take precaution to know how to change when necessary. The slight changes that you make will make all the difference in the world.

***

Conclusion

Moving in a certain direction in a certain way is important, but we need to have selective persistence. We need to know that we are being smart in our persistence and our effort toward enlightenment.

We need both a target to shoot for and intensity by which we need to aim for and focus on. We must look in the mirror and see our weak self and strive to improve. Knowing that it will be hard and arduous but that it could be done by rewiring our brain to be positive.

We need to be shooting for incremental improvement when we change our daily approach to enlightenment. We cannot keep doing what we always have done.

If you change your approach, and attempt to set stretch goals, then you will be forced to use creativity and innovation. Incremental changes will help you prosper. Success is a continuous target, and we have to work at it. If we do, then success is imminent.

Take on a new set of risks. Like the fly hitting off the top of the open container, we tend to start weighing the losses heavier than the potential gains. The fly cannot manifest the escape mechanism, but you can by rewiring your brain through neuroplasticity.

Good vibrations are offering you the power to radiate harmonic energy through gratitude and kindness.

Whatever you want to manifest, be at peace of mind, be content and have the right intentions, respecting the good that you already have.

Remember you need both direction and intensity to succeed. Choose the right direction and incorporate the fortitude of intensity to reach enlightenment. Be ready to receive your good fortune with gratitude. Happiness comes with the ability to be grateful for what you already have while manifesting what you really want.

***

CHAPTER 2

Emotional Moments
of Resonance

The only thing we have to fear is fear itself.

—*Franklin D. Roosevelt*

The one thing that all personal development experts agree upon is goal setting. Set goals but ensure that you make a presence in the moment. First, set a goal that you will achieve that is something that you strive for. Then add a process goal or an action plan to achieve that goal that you can do each day.

When you analyze your thoughts, you may wonder where they come from. You know that they come from your brain and all the experiences that impacted your life. Especially the last experience that you may have had just recently. The recency effect may be a huge determinant of your current thought process. Do not worry; that too shall pass.

Think about it as if your life is sculpture.

You are peeling off the surface that may cause you to feel negative thoughts. Replace your thoughts with your strong empowering thoughts. Killing the weak version that has been feeding you lies, and you can change these thoughts by replacing them by rewiring your brain.

Challenge a limiting belief by being aware of your thoughts, recognize it, then consciously think of a new thought. Thoughts like "I will never succeed," will change to "Every step I take I am getting closer to where I want to be in my life." Feel good about going into the new.

Look kindly on your thoughts and smile, accept them, but do not judge them, just realize they are a part of you, resist judgment. We tend to add negativity to our thoughts at the emotional level. Your mind has a component to it that is an untamed ego that develops over time and hijacks your present moment.

When we expect things to happen, we attract it subconsciously. Here comes the road rage. Here comes the insomnia. My relationship is bound to end like all the others did. Thoughts like this are unnecessary but they may be part of you, and you may have to deal with them. You can say STOP or CANCEL but those techniques are outdated. That approach places more emphasis on the thought itself. Just accept it, and let it go. Say to yourself, "This too shall pass."

Letting go of past stress and heartache is important for your resonance. It will help you to be your best self.

Resonance is the ability to evoke or suggest images, memories, and emotions. Your resonance is usually developed from your accumulated past, and, in some cases, it provides negative energy and draws on your emotions and occupies your body and mind. We carry narratives about ourselves without even knowing it. To truly act, you must begin to rewrite these internal narratives or stories that are limiting your potential. You must shift your identity and reshape your mind by consciously choosing the right thoughts.

Attempt to shift to aligned with what you want, not what you do not want. You see yourself as deserving what you seek. You do not need to be validated by others. Become authentic and manifest your desires that help you to change how you see yourself. You are not forcing anything; you are becoming more of who you truly are. You allow things to flow to you naturally. Do not be needy because that shows lack. Instead, focus on completeness just as you are.

Material things will not provide what you need. You are not deficient, when you act from a place of abundance you get more of what have right now. React from a place in which you already have what you want and release the neediness. Great things flow naturally into your life.

Doug Newberg, an authority on how to feel better about your life's journey argues that you have or had a dream and that is important to you.

Doug wrote a book with Jim Clawson, my colleague and friend, titled *Powered by Feel: How Individuals, Teams, and Companies Excel.* Doug asked over 850 students at University of Virginia, "How do you want to feel?" They never had been asked that before.

As you prepared for your dream you may have faced obstacles, but you can think of how you felt so passionate about your dream, and then think about how you want to feel now. Martin Luther King did not say I have a plan, I have a vision, he said "I have a dream!"

In many cases, you overcame those obstacles and in other situations perhaps you have not. You can either revisit your dream or you may be stuck in the *Have-To-Do* cycle.

Unload your excess baggage, lay out the contents, and unpack. Wake up and look in the mirror and say goodbye to the weak version of yourself that you do not recognize anymore. That person staring back at you is your weak version. It is necessary to change for your growth. You can transform yourself to be the best self that you can be.

Positive psychology can help you ascertain the life that you deserve. You can be the architect of your own life. It requires courage and determination. Step out of your comfort zone and let go of mediocrity and get to a place that you want to be. Get to that place in which you know how you really want to feel.

You become the person that you want to be, you feel confidence, and this confidence attracts things that you want into your life.

If you identify with yourself as successful, then you gravitate toward that as you align your actions, behaviors, and decisions that help you to become more successful. You carry yourself with a certain confidence and everyone sees that in you as a stronger more capable version of you. Coming from lack will only attract lack.

Alan Watts once related our past to a ship's wake. Watts is one of the greatest philosophers in the world. He died at 58 when being treated for a heart condition.

Alan said throughout his life, "Would you rather live a long life doing what you don't want to do, or live a short life doing what you want to do all the time?" Some feel that he died from alcohol abuse. He was a wise man, one who knew how to look at the existence of the world and perhaps this was his way to deal with reality in his own eyes. We can still learn a great deal from him.

Watts argues that, when thinking of a ship, a cruise, or even on a small boat, the wake is always behind you. The wake can never drive the ship so why is it that your wake in your life is impacting your resonance. The key with mindsense is to **Know Thyself!**

> *Self-knowledge leads to wonder, and wonder leads to curiosity and investigation, so that nothing interests people more than people, even if only one's own person. Every intelligent individual wants to know what makes him or her tick, and yet is at once fascinated and frustrated by the fact that oneself is the most difficult of all things to know.* —The Book: On the Taboo Against Knowing Who You Are (Alan Watts, 1966, pp. 139–140)

As Bruce Lee, the great Chinese kung fu fighter, once said: "Fat Belly Never Knows Hunger." This is true. If you do not like what you see in the mirror, then you are dwelling on the weak or negative version of yourself. Unfortunately, your approach to resonance will be tainted.

Turn it around by instantly getting up and going for a 15-minute walk which will end up being 30 minutes when you turn around and head back. Smart phones can count your steps. You cannot imagine how many steps you take in a day, even if you are cleaning your home.

See the image of yourself that you do not want to see and explore the aspects of your life in which this weak self exists, then develop strategies to stop the weak version and bring out a stronger more perceptive version.

You are good enough, you deserve success, you can take risks. Your potential is limitless.

Visualize yourself as the person that you want to be and push past your comfort zone.

Be aware of your thoughts. Recognize your old, outdated pattern of yourself.

Say to yourself: "I can do this say, I got this, I am capable of learning and growing."

Scientists have found that the brain does not know the difference when you visualize your ideal self, and you see it and you feel the pride, feel the joy of having what you want, and the sense of accomplishment. Visualization alone is not enough; you need to add action to align with your vision. You cannot think yourself out of a rut. You must have intent; Intention gets you to the better version of yourself.

Like a snowball rolling down a hill, you will develop into a stronger version of yourself with mindsense and you will have better resonance.

Your thoughts are solidified when you continuously identify with them either semi consciously or subconsciously. You can never get enough of what you do not want. Do not focus on driving out the negative, focus on adding the positive thoughts to replace the old ones.

Goal setting is done in the current moment. Quieting your mind is what is called strategic silence; it could involve meditation, or it could just be planning or working on something until you would like to let people know about it, like a book, or a relationship. Neville Goddard, in 1949, in his book *Out of This World*, argued that:

> *Dreams, and meditation, can help us first by noticing what we are desiring and then imagining that we are experiencing that which we desire to experience, we can match the future in harmony with our desire. Desire and imagination are the enchanter's wand of fable, and they draw to themselves their own affinities. They break forth best when the mind is sleeping or meditating. We are in control in the direction of our thoughts by wishing and assuming that our wish is fulfilled.*

Strategic silence or mediating can help your resonance level grow.

Do not live someone else's dream. If you find yourself alone, attempt to like who you are alone with, if you chose to be alone, then it is your choice.

Create the world you want. If you do not change something nothing will change. Be determined to change if you chose to do so.

Through your imagination, create a conscious mind impressed with who you want to be and place this in your mind through repetition. See yourself in love, see the job you want, see the car you want to drive, see the living quarters that you want to dwell in, and you will attract it. The mind can only record the feeling that you have and not whether you have it or not.

Placing precedence on personal development opens up the opportunity to thrive. Manifestation is real, it works. Steve Jobs, the renowned entrepreneur, says that connect the dots looking backward. See yourself in it to win it. Then win it.

Neville Goddard in his book *Awakened Imagination* argues that you must create the world in which you want. Unfortunately, you cannot not go backward. Keep on keeping on.

Going backward is something General Ulysses Grant never wanted to do, and General Lee had Grant on his toes because Lee was a better strategist in the Civil War.

> *Everyone has his or her superstitions. One of mine has always been when I started to go anywhere, or to do anything, never to turn back or to stop until the thing intended was accomplished*—Ulysses S. Grant

Our pickers are somewhat off, and we do not realize it until we are aware that we selected the wrong partner, the wrong job, or the wrong place to live. Ask yourself: "Why do I pick the wrong things in my life out of some recurring habit that is probably the old weak version of myself that needs to change?"

Work at your relationships, find a partner and not a project, and, most of all, do not feel that everyone is replaceable because they truly are not. Each fingerprint is made especially for each individual and no one is replaceable.

See yourself in the arms of the person of your dreams, see yourself in the company of your choice, the car you want to drive, the house you want to live in. Be there, feel it, and make it happen. Manifest it!

> *The future must become the present in the imagination of the one who would wisely and consciously create circumstances. We must translate vision into being. Your imagination must center itself in some state and view the world from that state*—**Neville Goddard**

Through enlightenment and mindsense you can consciously create the circumstances in life that you want.

When you think with the end in mind, see it fully, have a solid picture solidified in your mind, describe it with detail. It is not as hard as you think.

Describe what you want but you may not have in your possession right now.

The American philosopher, Eric Hoffer (1902–1983), is a rare thinker. He is a philosopher, and his books embody that indispensable quality that informs the thought of all great thinkers: he argues that intuition is a method to undertake as you manifest your destiny.

To learn you need a certain degree of confidence. Not too much confidence and not too little. If you have too little confidence, you will think that you cannot learn and grow. If you have too much confidence, you will think that you do not have to learn and grow—Eric Hoffer

Eric is referring to your ego. It will keep you from messing up and it will cause you to act as if you are much better than you actually are.

The ego holds you back to be safe or overextends you which may give you the impression to see a weakness or an inability in yourself. The ego tells you not to do that again and make a fool of yourself. Watch your ego. It may keep you in your place or it may overexpand your boundaries into areas that are not for you. Such as getting promoted to a position in which you are not qualified for.

If you are a manager or supervisor or want to become one, be careful because Laurence Peters, in his book, titled the *Peter Principle,* argued that all managers rise to an occasion in their career in which they fail. To avoid the Peter Principle, do not take on too much so that you are working so hard that you cannot enjoy your life. Attempt to get promoted at the right time and stay where you are when it is necessary to prolong your career and enjoy it.

Finding your purpose in life is important. Your reason to get out of bed in the morning and begin your day matters.

A desire to enjoy your work or professional life is key to motivate you to live in the moment upon waking up in the morning. Knowing you will have a fun day ahead doing what you love or being around the people that you care about, will keep you in a good mood. Just waking up to the smell of a good cup of coffee, cherishing these moments are important for you mindsense.

Napoleon Hill felt that desire creates ability. If you wake up in the morning and say all I want to do is pay my bills, you will not be motivated.

Our Ego wants us to create what Wayne Dyer calls "Earth Goals Only." Earth goals are important but when you add universal goals, you can manifest much more. The universe does not care about you, but it will care about you if you tap into it and use it to your advantage.

Remember that time when you attempted to forget something like a phone number. Sometimes you may have dialed it without thinking. Eventually, the number subsided from your thoughts. That is the universal power helping you move on with your life.

Begin to experience positive emotions and you will have a stronger resonance.

In the movie called *Midnight Run*, with Charles Grodin and Robert DeNiro. Charles played the character of the criminal, and accountant, and DeNiro, played an ex-cop that was divorced from his wife, a bounty hunter. DeNiro caught Charles and was taking him into custody.

Charles wanted to know what time it was. He began to become familiar with DeNiro and noticed he had a watch on his wrist.

"What time it is, Jack," Charles asked DeNiro.

"The watch does not work," DeNiro answered as if uncaring.

"Why are you wearing a watch that does not work?" Charles asked with an inquisitive auditor look in his eye.

"My ex-wife gave it to me, and it has sentimental value," said DeNiro with a slight sense of loneliness and regret.

"It is time to get rid of the watch, Jack!"

We carry thoughts the same way by letting them fester when we realize they exist because we keep nurturing them. If you stop feeding the thought, it will dissipate.

The Origin of Fear. Fear is false evidence appearing real. Roosevelt put it nicely in his inaugural address for the President of the United States, "Only Thing We Have to Fear Is Fear Itself."

Franklin D. Roosevelt wanted to remind Americans that the nation's "common difficulties" concerned "only material things," and that these material things are in our mind as a continuous problem that we create and reciprocate. We create danger in our minds that does not exist.

We should avoid unnecessary danger, but we cannot always worry about it, or we will never leave our homes.

In your lifetime, a terrible thing, like 911, brought the possibility and probability closer in your mind. We do not know why things like this happen, but we must attempt to stay positive and think good thoughts.

Peter Daniels, a motivational speaker, once said that self-preservation is important, but it must not impede your daily routine. He noticed that his wife liked strawberry preserves. This caused him to wake up before her and make her toast with butter and strawberry preserve along with coffee. This he called it self-preservation because he met a need for his wife and showed her how much he cared about not only her but preserving his marriage. Sometimes we have to put a humorous spin on our life and livelihood.

Psychological fear is created in our brain and comes to us through our thoughts. Past problems, issues that we remember that are negative, seep through to our daily thought pattern. This thought process seeps into our conscious mind, our thinking, and our self-awareness or self-concept. It can be a menial thought that really does not matter much but it lodged deep in our brain and occurs at different times. The thought is usually associated with someone meaningful in some way in our life. This is very common.

To change our self-concept, we must reprogram our subconscious. The subconscious does not know the difference between reality and unreality. It simply takes what you give it as facts. Being a victim of your own thought patterns could add negative connotations. To gain Mindsense, you must reprogram your subconscious and move toward the direction of positive thoughts, which could be your true north.

Abraham Lincoln, the U.S. president that saved the Union and abolished slavery, once said during a scene of the movie *Lincoln*, based on the book *Team of Rivals* by the presidential historian Doris Kearns Goodwin.

A compass, I learned while I was surveying, it will point you true north from where you are standing but it does not provide advice about the swamps, deserts, and rivers that you will encounter along the way. If in pursuit of your destination you plunge ahead heedless of obstacles and achieve nothing more than to sink in a swamp, then what is the use of knowing true north— Abe Lincoln

Surround yourself with positive people. Positive people will build your self-esteem when they are supportive and caring.

Geese provide great lessons on teamwork. They fly in a V-format and switch out of the lead role when tired. The geese at the back honk to encourage the lead goose. Surround yourself around people that act like the geese do and honk for you with encouragement.

When your mind is at peace, you realize that you are safe now and should not worry about what will happen in the future. The same with marriage. If the word divorce gets a lot of airtime, then divorce may be more likely to happen.

The past has warts, and the future is undetermined, so you have to live in the present moment.

Most of your thoughts are centered on your values–assumptions– beliefs–and expectations (VABEs); your VABES are about how you see the world and how the world should be.

The events in your life or your future expectations are what you create in your mind based upon your VABES. Everyone experiences some feelings of anxiety and stress at times. This is a natural part of our life cycle. If you let your anxiety rule you, then your ego is getting the best of you. The future may be riddled with enough problems and anxiety, and there is no need to be concerned about that in the present moment.

You can use the *CLOP* model to *control* your thoughts, *lead* yourself, *organize* your life, and *plan* your day. What you do right now is all that matters; when the future arrives, you may have to go back to the *CLOP* model so that you feel in control of your life at that moment.

Don't let your ego rule your life.

The ego is the Zorro of your life. Zorro took from the rich and gave to the poor, but he felt that he had good reason. The story of Zorro shows how ego could take over one's life. The difference between Zorro and you is that you have so much more in your favor in our modern society filled with opportunities. Letting your ego get the best of you is futile to your well-being. We must keep our ego intact to catch our mind before we lose it.

Vignette—The Story of the Real-Life Zorro

The Story of the Real-Life Zorro, Joaquin Murrieta. Like so many other men during the California Gold Rush, Joaquin Murrieta traveled to the mountains in the hopes that he could earn lots of money. He was just 18 years old at the time. He was young, bright-eyed, ambitious, and completely in love with his young wife. They wanted to have a family together, and he promised to find lots of gold, while his wife took care of their little house.

Since he was one of the first people to pan for gold in that area, he truly was making a lot of money, and they had no reason to want to pack it up early and go home. If he stayed long enough, he could gather enough gold to be a very rich man. He and his wife likely celebrated every time he came home with a new cache of gold, and they would dream of the future under the stars.

Unfortunately for Murrieta, he ran into some very bad timing. In 1848, that area of California was won by the United States in the Mexican–American War.

One day, American men approached Murrieta and his wife at their home and demanded that he hand over his gold and his mining plot. They said that the land was their territory now, and all Mexicans needed to leave. When Murrieta refused to give up his plot, the men tied him up to a chair and forced him to watch while they tortured and sexually abused his wife. He had to watch her die from her injuries before he finally escaped from the ropes that tied him down.

The men left him alive, probably because they would never believe such a young man could do anything to retaliate. He buried his wife and returned to his hometown alone.

He returned to his village with a broken heart and empty pockets.

He tried to become a card dealer in a saloon, working with the drunk American men he secretly hated so much. One day, his half-brother got a new horse, and he borrowed it to ride into town. A group of American men stopped him and whipped him, saying that he was a horse thief. Murrieta blurted out the horse was not stolen, and that he borrowed it from his brother.

When they heard this, they found his brother and lynched him in the town square as a horse thief, even though he was innocent. The Americans had killed not just one but two of the closest people in Joaquin Murrieta's life.

All around him, he witnessed Mexican people who were born and raised in California getting tortured and persecuted by White men. This flicked a switch in his brain that took him from being a good, ambitious young man to one who was hell-bent on getting revenge.

Zorro wore a mask, wielded a cape and a sword, and he announced his presence by slashing the letter Z on a wall, sort of like modern-day graffiti. Like the legendary English outlaw Robin Hood, Zorro robbed from the rich and gave to the poor. The only difference between Robin Hood and Zorro is that Zorro was Hispanic.

***

Unlike Zorro's ego, which is understanding that he had a reason to be aggressive, your ego is very vulnerable and insecure, and it makes you feel that you are constantly under threat.

Zorro lost everything. His ego took over and he felt that lawlessness was his destiny.

You too may be feeling a fear of loss, a fear of failure, a fear of hurricanes, earthquakes, tornados, wild animals, and even, perhaps, thieves in the night. Fear is the ego's way of making a person feel that they may be dying early in life. Granted, we hear many stories of this happening, but the chance of dying early should not be a concern. To the ego, death is always knocking at your door like the big bad wolf who wants to blow your house down in the story "The Three Little Pigs." The big bad wolf only blew the weak house down and that is why we build our house on rock and not sand.

When someone goes against your way of thinking, instead of trying to be right, you can consider the possibility of being wrong even if it goes against your ego. Take the high road and agree to disagree on certain things.

If you feel strongly about something, you can still believe it or verify it later for your own sake, but do not let the ego get you into an argument.

You can be an authentic self-leader without having the ego telling you that you must be right all the time. That should not matter to you.

Edward Welch wrote a book with an interesting title, *What Do You Think of Me? Why Do I Care?* Welch felt that peer pressure, codependency, shame, low self-esteem—these are just some of the words used to identify how people are controlled by other people's opinion. We all must be prepared to avoid the emotional hijackings that people draw us into such as but not limited to anger, fear, depression, anxiety, and apathy. Using Mindsense makes you much better at avoiding people that may try to hijack your life.

A recent article in Harvard Business Publishing Education suggests that many of us are teetering on the edge of burnout and cannot exactly pinpoint why, coining a phrase "microstress" as a culmination of a million things. They seem small and manageable but cumulatively they can take an enormous toll and lead to overthinking. A couple of tips offered to avoid microstress are:

1. Start small—narrow down and tackle a single source of microstress to help build confidence and adjust your mindset.
2. Recognize the impact of draining relationships—fight the urge to automatically lend yourself to a person close to you, even if it makes you feel good at the moment.
3. Be attuned to the microstress you cause—try to pinpoint where you can make adjustments that will lead to more positive conversations.
4. Get involved with activities that give you a greater sense of purpose—to achieve a multidimensional life, try to find ways to connect with others that are compatible.

Rob Cross, in his book *The Hidden Toll of Microstress*, explains how stress can be complicated, but with an awareness of how to deal with stress you can free yourself of being overwhelmed with day-to-day actions.

A *Harvard Business Review* article published in February 2024, by Cross, Dillon, and Martin, titled "5 Ways to Deal with the Microstresses Draining your Energy," offers a path to deal with the everyday stress that entails much of our lives.

- Change your mindset
- Create positive interactions
- Be resilient
- Share interactions with people
- Derive a greater sense of purpose

As mentioned early, Wayne Dyer talks about "Earth Goals Only" (EGO). Planning goals based on your ego may steer you wrong because it searches for the mediocrity.

The egoic mind is causing you to do things in an obligatory way. You have a choice to make when selecting your goals and breaking them down to smaller goals will help. The ego will try to hold you back, keep you safe, and get you to not take risks. Mihaly Csikszentmihalyi (2009;2016) described FLOW as an immersive state of "optimal experiences," capturing the very essence of flow and offering a potential path to meaningful happiness.

What you do is secondary to how you do it because when you are in FLOW, you are deeply involved in your craft. FLOW helps you to live in the moment. Wherever you are, you want to be there. For now, think of FLOW as doing what you want in life.

Jim Clawson, an emeritus professor of leadership and organizational behavior at the Darden School of Business, at the University of Virginia, coined the term *Level Three Leadership*. He identified three levels that can help you with Mindsense. Jim's three levels consists of Level One, which is what you do and usually is driven by your ego. Level Two: Jim found that we use our conscious thought to help us massage the ego to do things in a practical and knowledgeable way. Level Two consists of knowledge and is based on data that we obtained or our expertise that we learned in school or training sessions. Jim opens up a greater channel of mindsense, Level Three, which is doing things with our semiconscious or unconscious behavior.

Jim found that most of the things we do on a habitual basis are at Level Three and sometimes we are unaware of why we are doing certain things. Understanding these three levels of human behavior tames the ego and gives you the most potential for success.

Level Three self-leadership homes in on your VABES, which are your *values, assumptions, beliefs, and expectations of how the world is or how the world should be*. At this level, you achieve greatness and unleash the power of the ego to your advantage.

At Level One and Level Two, the ego will tell you that you ought to do things in a certain way, but the things done at these levels are not worthy or good enough for any type of success. The reason for this is that they are more manipulative and based on rewards and threats, even to ourselves.

At Level Three, the ego will only be felt indirectly as an intense craving, and innate desire that you want or need. This will give you a sense of compliance with your thoughts and keep you from feeling anxious.

When you are driven by your ego at Level One or Level Two, you may enter into a compulsive pursuit of ego gratification such as drinking alcohol, promiscuity, gambling, and overeating. The alcoholic passes a saloon and has to go in because he or she is drawn into it. A gambler keeps thinking of the next card game, the next slot machine, or the next trip to Las Vegas. The is an innate draw to a person's internal desire.

There are many people that strive for more. More status in their career, more possessions, more money, and more success of any form. Some seek power over others, recognition in any form, or a special personal relationship that they must have or do not want to lose. In some instances, once ascertained, people feel happier and as if they have arrived at the place that they want to be in life, and in other cases, people still feel as if they need something else. We often hear about some cases, such as a person winning the lottery that has led to their demise. By looking for happiness in the future we are rejecting the present moment.

The gambler does not always want to win; it is the feeling of playing and the internal need to see if they will win that drives them. Some people reach the pinnacle of their accomplishment, but even when they obtain all these material things, they often find something missing, a desire that is unfed and leaving a hole that is still there, a bottomless pit, a quicksand.

Maxwell Maltz, a plastic surgeon, discovered that even if he can augment a scar on someone's face through plastic surgery, the person would see the perfection but still feel empty inside. He coined the word "psycho-cybernetics" as a way to help people change from the inside.

Maltz, The Man, The Myth, The Magic

Maxwell Maltz (March 10, 1899–April 7, 1975) was an American cosmetic surgeon and author of Psycho-Cybernetics (1960), which was a system of ideas that he claimed could improve one's self-image leading to a more successful and fulfilling life. He wrote several books, among which Psycho-Cybernetics was a long-time bestseller—influencing many subsequent self-help teachers. His orientation toward a system of ideas that would provide self-help is considered the forerunner of the now popular self-help books.

According to Maltz, before the mind can work efficiently, you must develop your perception of your outcomes that you expect to reach. When the mind has a defined target (psycho-cybernetics), it has a better chance to focus on the target until you reach your intended goal.

Mindsense encourages you to be an inside-out type of person instead of an outside-in type person. Accomplish what you want and select a career you love. Do what you love as much as possible.

Conclusion

To find emotional moments of resonance, set goals that you know you can accomplish, set goals that you think that you can do, and, most importantly, set goals that you have no idea how to accomplish but you know that if you try hard enough, you will.

Habit stack by building habits into already built-in habits. Making coffee gives you a few moments to plan your day, meditate, or just breathe with mindsense.

If you stay at Level One self-leadership, the ego mind will continue to run your life, and you will be constantly on the go to meet the ego needs. My mom, Ann Provitera, would always say: "I just want peace of mind, Son." This is the same as taming the ego.

Peace of mind is your way of controlling your ego from running your life. Without peace of mind, you cannot be at ease, and you cannot be at peace. The ego offers spurts of satisfaction but nothing that is lasting and truly fulfilling.

The ego will always get you if you let it because it is derived from external things based upon the outside-in, usually materialistic things. It may cause you to live above your means because the ego has no remorse. The ego needs to be supported, wants to be nurtured, and must be fulfilled on a continuous basis. If you let your ego identify you, you will continue to search for more possessions.

There is nothing about you that has changed when you meet the needs of the ego because it is all driven from a desire to achieve something more instead of accepting what you have and enjoying it.

It makes mindsense to take an inventory of what you already have and be grateful.

Look at the loved ones next to you and those that are dear to you, including pets. Sit with them in the same room, travel with them, and revel in just being without the need of satisfying the ego. This is where the heart and soul belong.

***

CHAPTER 3

Moments in Your Ship's Wake

The future depends on what you do today.

—Mahatma Gandhi

Discipline is the bridge between goals and accomplishment

—Jim Rohn

Alan Watts, an English writer and lecturer (1915–1973), asked: "What in your Wake?"

Watts noted that a ship's wake is something that is left behind. Others may know the boat's wake as a disturbing nuisance to intracoastal waterways. The wake, or in this case, your past, can never drive the ship. Your thoughts of the past can never drive your direction forward and can only hold you back even thinking about them.

As we drive on highways, we see skid marks on the road. Some deep and long, some short and dull. One may wonder what happened when that car skidded. Although we see the skid marks in front of us, what happened is in the past. Even if you skid, you cannot look back or care, too. You are concerned about what is in front of you.

Same with the wake of your past; it is always going to be behind you and should not disrupt your present moment.

Mindsense does not ensure that you can control your thoughts, but it does allow you to manage or deal with them when they occur.

Do not let your thoughts fester, just realize that you must have had something good, or bad, happen to you that continues to bring it up in your mind. Your mind and memory are feeding you thoughts all the time. The thoughts will dissipate over time. Let the thoughts be.

Your memory is filled with long lost dreams, personality defective things that happened to you, and past relationships that come to mind in your thoughts and are unmanageable in the present moment.

Two things that come up in your present moment are joy and happiness. If you are not feeling joy in your life, that could cause you to feel dull and vapid at the present moment. Happiness is something you either have or not. Abe Lincoln said either you are happy or not, either way, you are right. That is why we seek peace of mind now or in the near future. Feeling joy and happiness is your mantra.

If you let the past bother you, then you are letting your wake bother you, and you will feel stuck in a world that no longer exists. If you let the near or extended future bother you, you lock on to despair of doubt and discouragement. You lock on to the negative thoughts and lock out happy thoughts in the present moment. On one side of the spectrum, you may feel anxiety but on the other, more extreme, side you could feel that you are full of despair and depression.

Wayne Dyer once said that if you do not like being alone, then you do not like who you are alone with. If you are preoccupied with a past, you approach life as Eeyore in *Winnie the Pooh*.

Living in a current fog exemplifies Linus van Pelt, a major character in Charles M. Schulz's comic strip *Peanuts*. Linus is a continuously belittled by his colleagues over his security blanket. Your security blanket is riddled with doubt about your current potential if you continuously believe that the future is flawed, and you hold on to it.

Bill Gove is one of the most trusted names in the professional speaking industry. Bill says, "If I want to be free, I have got to be me." As you build your talent, your confidence comes from your knowledge. Build your knowledge and confidence base and you will see how your competence also increases. You want to develop a calm confidence in front of people. This will help you in the moments shared with others and build mindsense.

Wallace Wattles was an American writer who wrote a book in 1910 titled *The Science of Getting Rich*; he argued that money is a necessary commodity, while Mark Twain felt that "Money is the root of all evil, but it sure does solve a lot of problems." Wattles agreed with Twain, in that money should not drive your life, but having enough can result in much less problems in life.

Do all the work you can do, every day, and do each piece of work in a perfectly successful manner; put the power of success, and the purpose to get rich, into everything you do—**Wallace Wattles**

Mindsense is not written to get you rich; it is written to help you achieve enlightenment, an essence of being that makes living a life of enjoyment, but, along the way, if you collect enough money to be happy, more power to you.

Everyone should have a decent standard of living to live comfortably and pursue their goals. Live in a city that is less expensive so that you can foster your dreams and build your goals.

Rhonda Byrne used Wattles book as an inspiration for her best-selling book and the film *The Secret*. The movie is about manifestation and using positive psychology.

Doing what you love has always been a mantra of mine. L. P. Jacks argued that if you love what you do, then you never work a day in your life. Earl Nightingale agrees with Jacks in that you do not go to work for money, but rather you go to work for satisfaction. When you provide a service, you earn the money to live and prosper. John Wayne once mentioned in a cowboy movie scene that he does not pay a man for his work. Wayne said: "I give anybody anything that works for me. The man puts in the day's work and the man gets paid a day's wage." Whatever your hands touch, do it with all your might and experience in an effort to continuously improve.

Your success comes from a worthy ideal that you feel is important. Your success begins where you are at in the present moment, and in that moment, you plan where you are going. While you are in the current moment, enjoying whatever you are doing, take the time to connect the ideas that come up in your mind with your future. When you get to that future, which will also be a moment, you will be there to act at that time.

Change the way you reach your goals and create new habits in your daily moments to make your future brighter. Tangible things like money and assets are all good things to aspire to ascertain. Tangible things are important for survival, but it is the intangible things that matter most, which are love, family, and friends.

Some people are concerned about what others think of them. This is an individual issue that may impact you. Mindsense argues that you should not worry about what someone else thinks of you. In many instances, it is not your problem; they own the problem.

Terry Cole-Whittaker in her book title states, *What You Think of Me Is None of My Business.* Do not worry about what someone thinks of you. Unless it is your boss or significant other, then it truly does not matter to your well-being. Earl Nightingale said that if you know how little other people were thinking, you would not be concerned with what they are thinking.

Keep your life on purpose and focus on the moments of your day. Each moment matters. Spend the moments wisely. Focus on your own thinking. Think positive and walk around with a chip on your shoulder. You have everything you need to succeed right now.

You are not what you think. People have recurring thoughts about important things, unimportant things, and things that they may not like about themselves. For instance, a deprived child that used to steal money from their parents may continually deal with the urge to steal. However, upon some success in life, that young child grows to be a successful adult that does not need to steal for a living.

People who have vices attempt to improve their current moment with outside substances. Unfortunately, the improvement comes with a downside, which is usually a hangover or loss of brain cells.

Brain cells are fascinating, and we sometimes take them for granted. Your mind is like the new threat of artificial intelligence; it is overpowering, overbearing at times, and intrusive. At the same time, your mind is the most powerful organ in your body and using it to live an enlightened life with essence and presence is the way of mindsense. You are much better than artificial intelligence.

My friend Jim Clawson often refers to childhood development and how it impacts leaders. The mind develops quickly as an infant. At birth, the human brain is growing at the rate of 250,000 cells per minute. During the first year of a human life, approximately 90 percent of nutrition goes to the brain. In lieu of approximately 100 billion brain cells, each of these cells connects to ten or so thousand other cells. Could exceed a quadrillion synaptic connections. From birth, our minds, for the most part, are developed perfectly.

The mind certainly is fascinating, but it may also get in your way at times. I know when I see a full moon, I feel a certain energy, just as the myth of a werewolf getting energized during the full moon. The Native Americans placed a precedence on time and the full moon, and they would negotiate under the moon and stars. Three moons would equal 3 months. The explorers of the State of Florida used the stars to navigate the ocean in search of the fountain of youth, which can be found in St. Augustine, Florida. A planetarium show explains this quite interestingly.

When using mindsense, your mind is a tool to help you navigate through life. It is an organ or a mechanism to help you complete a task, plan an endeavor, protect you from unexpected circumstances, but through nonsense the mind is often wasted.

Henry Mintzberg, a leadership guru in Canada, coined self-knowledge or self-awareness is one of the most important self-leadership characteristics in a *Harvard Business Review* article. Consider yourself as leading yourself and already having a state of being with both self-knowledge and self-awareness.

Using positive psychology to feel the momentum of becoming your best self. Understanding how your mind works to your advantage and how it helps you deal with your mind effectively and efficiently is an important focal point for your well-being.

You think, you feel, you act in the present moment. Sometimes your present moments are dull, and you feel alone. Especially after the loss of a loved one, partner, or recent breakup. The reason for this is that our subconscious is filled with many good memories that are out of our control, and although we do not actually know what is taking hold of our subconscious, it impacts our thought process moment to moment. I remember when my mom died. Wow, that was a real kicker, she was the best thing that ever happened to me and gave me everything a mother could. Great cheer leader and wonderful woman.

If you feel sad after a loss of love, it is because you had a wonderful relationship and loved someone dearly. You can expect sad thoughts for many moments after losing someone dear to you.

Our ego may try to deflect and make us act strong, but it is OK to cry and be sad. I remember my dad saying that when his mom died, he tried not to cry because he wanted to be strong and manly. We do not have to be strong for other people; we need to be strong for ourselves.

Some subconscious memories could be from trauma that you experienced as a young baby, a toddler, or a young adult. Sure, you were in that moment when it happened, and it may have been traumatic, but that moment is gone now. The thoughts may appear; accept them.

Take care of your current moment. Take positive action in the current moment or just relax. Mindsense is not about giving up goals and aspirations for the current moment; that would be too selfish.

Mindsense is about making the current moment your best friend and attaching your hopes and dreams to it and then enjoying it accordingly. This makes mindsense.

Vignette—Humpty Dumpty

Humpty Dumpty, introduced in *Mother Goose's Nursery Rhymes* in which most children first heard the rhyme. The story of Humpty Dumpty is based on a cannon used by the Royalists during the English Civil War. The cannon was positioned on the walls of Colchester. When the Parliamentary forces damaged the walls, the cannon fell to the ground.

> Humpty Dumpty sat on a wall,
> Humpty Dumpty had a great fall.
> All the king's horses and all the king's men
> Couldn't put Humpty together again.

What if Humpty Dumpty could be put back together again. Why is such a sad tale told to youngsters? Imagine Humpty Dumpty could be put back together again. We, as imperfect individuals, with all our flaws and defects want to believe that we can be put back together again.

Life is created as a system of challenging us to do more with less, spend more than we have, and achieving more than we should. We must realize that we are more than enough just who we are.

The belief that Humpty Dumpty was incomplete and could not be put back together again is a myth. Synonymous with our own mind telling us through our thoughts that we had a regretful past and we should have anxiety about our future.

The missing piece for Humpty Dumpty was inadequacy that is a fallacy. When we look at Humpty Dumpty as fixable, we begin to see his worth and capability.

Shedding the layers of false narratives that Humpty Dumpty cannot be put back together again is the same way we need to change the way we feel about ourselves. All your doubts and fears and self-inflicted limitations are all false assumptions. Don't let the thoughts coming from your memory distort your present moment.

All that you have done up to this point to improve yourself, all that you do now to continuously improve, will, at some point, be the reason that you are selected for something great. In the country of Germany, a German resume, called a Lebenslauf, is very similar to a traditional American resume. they use a resume as a life-walk, meaning that it covers from birth to the current date of their life. From your birth to now, you accomplished so much. Feel great right where you are. Just like change is constant so is the future. Success and happiness are yours right where you are.

Your past and your future have no impression on what you are going to do right. Unless you decide to use your past knowledge and experience for what you are doing at the moment. Your future plans and the direction you would like to head toward could also be planned in the current moment. Just as a rainbow may give hope and reflection it is just a mirage that you cannot grasp, it's a reflection, a prism. Just be who you are right now; you are enough.

Feel the presence of being. If you do, then you will begin to realize that your presence and your essence are one and the same. Be free of any doubt or internal belief that may hold you back. You are great just who you are, and you are so special. One of a kind. Be that person. Unique and authentic.

Spirituality is beyond the scope of this book. I am an Adrian Dominica Sisters Associate and follow the Dominican Catholic Order, which was founded by Saint Dominic, and I strive to be like Saint Dominic. He was always cheerful and pleasant—a comforter of positive psychology; he was patient, merciful, and kind to everyone he encountered. Embracing some sort of spirituality is something that is encouraged.

The one thing that all species have in common is the fight-or-flight instinct. Humans know this but select to not use it on occasion. Animals may use it because it is ingrained in their nature. When trouble surfaces upon us, we forget everything in our past and only consider the moment and how to react, if necessary. When cows get sick, they tend to just give up and some humans may be the same way. Perhaps cows are programmed to feel that they are made to be slaughtered and eaten, while humans may feel that there is a better afterlife.

Mindsense suggests that in life-threatening situations, the shift to being fully in the moment and using all your senses and being fully alert is necessary. The alertness happens naturally as a protective measure. We think quickly and effectively, right, or wrong we may react due to our instinct for survival. This stillness we experience, coupled with alertness, is our highest consciousness.

Like Bruce Lee, the famous Chinese kung fu artist, when he acted like a cat ready to strike and claw at moment's notice. A cat playing with claws-in with you is a sign of love for you. Your reaction when in a dangerous state comes from a state of full consciousness at that moment, an instinctive thought.

Courageous people add a fear factor. There are some people that seek the euphoric feeling of danger which is similar to a gambler wanting to gamble despite knowing there is a strong chance of losing. For them, they are programmed to gamble. The same with drugs. Many people like heroine but the conscious elation is momentary as they drift off into unconsciousness. Some people that take drugs cannot cope with reality—when reality is all we have.

Embracing the power of Mindsense can offset these compulsive feelings that place us in despair or alter our consciousness. It could be a daily log, or it could be just relaxing all day and doing nothing on the couch. No matter what you call it, look at your time with gratitude, and be in that moment.

When we give a minute of silence for someone, we take a moment out of our busy lives for that person. You will see the duration of a minute feels like a long time. That is how special your present moment actually is. It is your precious time; don't waste it. Your time is valuable. The timeless dimension of the moment.

You have the capacity to become magnanimous. You laugh, you cry, you smile, you feel the presence, and you are happy—this attracts people into your life. Do not let your ego control you. Master the art of strategic silence.

Reprogramming your subconscious is at the heart of personal development. The clock time that causes you to be consistent and persevere in your current endeavors is our mechanism to continuously focus on personal development. Our true north is our compass that determines the direction you are heading. Learning to cherish that alone time is important in your quest to be enlightened.

When you have someone in your life that you care for, nurture that relationship. Do not be a narcissist; ensure a positive connection. Be real and be caring.

Taking the good with the bad is important, but when the bad overrides the good, you may find yourself in a codependency type relationship. Thus, spend time in the present moment and think about your relationships—the ones that work, the ones that don't. Set boundaries.

The present moment and thought cause an awareness that is exactly what you need for survival. No matter what anyone tells you, whatever behavior is espoused, the one thing human beings have in common is that they all feel that they are the most important person on earth.

When in the present moment, take care of what you need to take care of for yourself and feel the tensions and stress that may occur, then just acknowledge it and let it pass. For instance, paying off credit card debt or planning a trip provides a sense of accomplishment and relief.

Persevering toward accomplishments. Do not let anyone stop you from achieving your destiny. If the past provides a sense of stress, take the present moment to plan better on how to make a better choice in the future. Setting goals and using a to-do list, rating some goals as a must-do, should-do, and perhaps-do are important. Work toward them at your leisure in the next future current moment. Learn from the past and take the appropriate action on the basis of your predictions of what would be a better choice using your personal discernment in the moment.

Develop a purpose in life and pursue it. The present moment remains as the essential factor of your life. Not just now but forever. Any lesson from the past becomes only relevant to your present when you cause it to be by dwelling on it. See how you feel in the present moment. If you feel restless, you may be harboring an old thought or you are with the wrong person. Just sit with someone. Never stop trying to find happiness and stay in the moment.

When achieving a particular goal, look at all the options and do not try to make something work that you have no control over. To be an enlightened person, your main focus is what you are doing right at that moment. Ask yourself, "What intention is most relevant right now?" Then go about it and do it. Even if it is to rest or to meditate.

We are always aware of time; however, it never slips by us, it just is and always will be until someday we run out of time altogether.

Mindsense frees you from the past and keeps you in the present moment of what is right now and who is important in your life at the present time.

All the psychological aspects of time matter. If you have a family, a pet, or simply nature, enjoy it and cherish that time. That makes you who you are in the present moment and who you will want to be in the future.

Mindsense is truly about finding your essence in life and becoming or improving upon your enlightenment.

One way to improve enlightenment is to look at the Big Five Index. The "Big Five" index refers to a widely accepted psychological model that describes personality traits using five broad dimensions: Openness, Conscientiousness, Extraversion (also often spelled extroversion), Agreeableness, and Neuroticism. These five dimensions are thought to encompass the most important aspects of personality and are used to understand individual differences.

- Openness. Be open to new adventures. Try new things but always remember to be in the moment. When I told my colleague and friend about writing a book about living in the moment, she said one word: "Passport." I laughed. Be open to travel.
- Conscientiousness. We attempt to be conscious all the time, but we also have a feeling of prior thoughts or future worries. In mindsense, the conscientious person selects companions wisely. Someone with mindsense, you know when to compliment people but also know when to compliment less. Create our own happiness in life by complimenting yourself.

- Extraversion. Being an extravert is not for everyone. There are people who are ambiverts. Ambiverts are people that can be introverted when necessary (i.e., Strategic Silence) but also can be extroverts when it is important to be with other people. In mindsense, we are very flexible. Mindsense helps us to think inside-out as opposed to outside-in.
- Agreeableness. Be aware of the downside to agreeableness. At one point, we must bow out gracefully and say a kind no to a person taking advantage of our good nature. Mindsense, for the most part, teaches us to be agreeable with boundaries.
- Neuroticism (also known as emotional instability). In some cases, in order to be great at something, we need to put a great deal of our time into practicing, learning, doing, and improving. It is important to learn, unlearn, and relearn. However, the neurotic person places to much emphasis on the past psychological time. Attempt to break free of the past as much as possible. Neuroticism could be preprogrammed in our minds that we replay in our head, and this impacts our current paradigm. A paradigm could be a model we play over in our mind. Mindsense teaches us to avoid neuroticism as much as possible.

The programs in our mind from childhood can seem to seep into our current thought process and obscure our productivity. If we find ourselves preprogrammed with a story in our mind, we must attempt to break free of this story in our mind and replace it with positive thoughts. Become a transcender and break away from the clutches of your past. Jim Clawson, a Harvard professor, once said:

> *Will you ever be anything more than a vessel transmitting the things that happen to you based upon previous generations on to the next? When you're no longer a defenseless child, will you ever become a transcender?— Jim Clawson*

The unenlightened consciousness ruins mindsense because our innovativeness and creativeness is tarnished. Our life loses purpose.

Wayne Dyer refers to this as our ego getting in the way of our accomplishments. When you only focus on your past failures or despair, your thought process and your life loses its enjoyment, lacks vitality, and prevents you from having a sense of wonder.

The old programs from childhood, adolescence, or adulthood, and the negative thoughts associated with these programs may lead to emotional despair, limiting your behavior, and this may cause you to have a delayed reaction to what is important in your life right now.

You may feel that you are accomplishing your goals but actually you may be acting out an endless repetition of what you lack and repeat performances that got you nowhere thus far. It's a failed movie script of your life that you are replaying in your mind. This behavior may distort your true potential.

With mindsense, you should not be covering up what you should be feeling in the current moment. Feel it but do not let it define you.

Negativity and suffering have their roots in time, but time is irrelevant. Action is a way of being persistent and achieving your goals with a disciplined mindset. We must drop the notion that the future is a replica of our past.

In many cases, your picker may be off. Review yourself often in the moment to see how you feel about yourself. If you feel negative, then you attract negative people. Feeling positive and happy attracts happy people. If you keep selecting the wrong people in your life, when they decide to leave you, you will feel a sense of relief. The relief comes from yourself for picking them in the first place.

Select the right people to be in your life, seek out the right significant others, create partnerships with people, and do not take on people as projects that need fixing.

Staying power is a unique trait and it works well for a good career and when you are in a good relationship.

John F. Kennedy once said,

If it is not necessary to change, it is necessary not to change

Selecting the right career is important and working at it to make the best of it by building on your competence is very important for your well-being as long as you do not be a career monger. Ensure to take time to develop good relationships with people while working hard at your career.

Transformation from past grief and hardship is possible for you. I think of my childhood with my dad, and I know that I had to reprogram some of the things that happened to me. I still have a visual of me locked in a car as a young boy waiting for him to come out of a house in which I did not know where or why he had gone, only to find out later that it was his mistress. Wow, that visual will be with me forever. To achieve your authentic self, you have to know these images in your mind exist and just move forward and reprogram that thought into love and kindness toward others.

Real change rarely occurs if you do not change the way you think about the past.

The Beatles sang the famous song ***LET IT BE*** for a reason. The song is a message of hope, urging the listener to accept whatever life brings them and to find peace in the midst of difficult situations. The lyrics suggest that everything will work out in the end and that it is important to stay positive and not give up. The band created some of the best lyrics in rock-and-roll history.

Through meditation and gratitude for the things that are tantamount in your life, such as your health, your loved ones, your pets, and your career, you can feel better about yourself and your life.

Transformation is possible as you become present in the current moment, and you can feel good about yourself in your own space. Accessing the current moment of peace, serenity, and tranquility is possible for you. Feel good about going into the new while enjoying where you are presently.

Many people do not realize that the time before their current moment is the cause of most of their current problems. If you get to this point in your life, the present moment is wasted on thoughts of the past that you have absolutely no control over.

We have many experiences in life, some we learn good things from and others we weed out the positive. Remember how great you really are, right now, at this moment.

Recognizing this pattern of thinking is your first step in understanding yourself and what makes you tick and leads to enlightenment. Your suffering can be stymied, and it does not matter what other people think or feel about your situation. Subconscious suffering is locked in your mind due to a traumatic past. Hypnosis or therapy may help but why not change the way your thoughts operate by monitoring the suggestions to yourself. Say I can, say I will, and say I am.

The problems in your past are real, but until you address them, acknowledge them, and deal with them, the dysfunctional thought process will continue to show its ugly face until you reprogram your thinking and that takes time. Address your past, relive it, then let it go.

If you do not face your problems head-on, you will find that even if you kicked the habit about thinking about that problem, another problem will surface. You may be attracting narcissistic people into your life because that is all you know, and you have not reprogrammed your thinking. You deserve better.

Vices are another problem; perhaps you gave up smoking cigarettes or vaping only to replace that positive change with another negative one. Even giving up drinking beer for nonalcoholic beer is not that much of a change. One time, Bob Scully, a colleague and best friend of mine for years, was in the hospital. It was St. Patrick's Day, so I stopped at Publix and bought balloons and O'Doul's nonalcoholic beer. When I got there his eyes lit up with the St. Patrick's Day spirit. The nurse told me that the beer still has a small percentage of alcohol in it and he could not drink it.

Mindsense creates a persona of kicking the habit and not replacing the habit with another one.

Your life situation is a temporary state that you find yourself in and it has been created by you. You are the solution to all your problems. No one can solve your problems but you.

If you are unhappy in your present moment, you are living in your past, or your negative opinion of your future. Denis Waitley put it mildly:

Dwell on the reward and you move toward it, dwell on the penalty and you move Toward IT!

Unhappiness is a systematic approach that you create in your mind. Your life situation is what it is. No one can make you happy without you making yourself happy first. The people that love you in your life may be the only people that truly care about you. The same goes with your pets that give unconditional love.

Time is right now; time is not in the past and time is not the future. This is your psychological happiness, and it is important to your well-being.

Three things make you feel psychological happiness: hope, bouncing back (resilience) from stress, and optimism.

One of the most important psychological aspects of mindsense is hope. Having hope is important to your well-being. Hope is key to your success because you must feel good about going into the new. Have hope but plan your next approach to improving your life because hope is not a strategy, it is a sentiment, for improving your life.

The second is resilience. Bouncing back is very important. You have to be aware of life's challenges because the older you get the more challenges that you will face. Believe that you can perform well in the present moment. You can also believe that your skills transfer well from job to job or from relationship to relationship. This way of thinking is called "self-efficacy"; it is the belief in the current moment that you can be good at something now and in the future in a similar situation. Feel great about going into the new with self-confidence and self-efficacy.

The third element of your success is optimism. Optimistic people live longer than pessimistic people. Price Pritchett asks the question: "Should you be less negative or more positive?" Most people say that they should be more positive, but in reality, it is the opposite: You need to be less negative in your moment-to-moment thinking of yourself.

Bruce Lee, the great Kung Fu philosopher once spoke about the power of speaking negative thoughts about oneself.

> *Don't speak negatively about yourself, even as a joke. Your body doesn't know the difference. Words are energy and cast spells, that is why it is called spelling. Change the way you speak about yourself, and you can change your life. What you are not changing you are also choosing*—Bruce Lee

My father, Frankie Prof, used to say, "No matter how bad things look at the time, Son, things always turn out to be for the best."

Goal setting is an important part of your life. A problem arises in the variation of goals and objectives either met or unmet. My dad also told me that when I failed at something, even the greatest plans between mice and men sometimes do not work out.

All problems have solutions. You must take your time, search with optimism, and treat all the people you encounter with the greatest respect, offering them unconditional love. Never ghost a person.

Look at Victor Frankl, a Holocaust survivor. He says that there are never problems, only situations to be dealt with. Until the situation changed for him, he had to deal with it accordingly. Frankl stated, "Happiness must happen, and the same holds for success: you have to let it happen by not caring about it until it does happen."

Frankl's "will" in life has roots in the meaning of life itself. This led him to write the book titled *Man's Search for Meaning*.

If you think of your problem right at this moment, you may find that there is no relevant problem. It is you thinking that you have a problem that may not even exist. Also, problems are sometime an impetus to go out and do something or try to ascertain or manifest something better. Thus, your solution to your problem is your answer. You come into this world alone and you leave this world alone. Your problems come in too with you and you have the fortitude to solve any problem when you put your mind to it.

Mindsense requires a quantum leap in the evolution of consciousness. Breaking negative patterns of the mind and the thoughts that subside when you live in the moment have been a problem for humans for centuries. Our genetic makeup can cause our mind to drag on the memes of our ancestors. We must transcend the negative strides of our ancestors and begin to develop what Price Pritchett calls a quantum leap.

As a leader of your own life, you not only think for yourself and your own well-being, but you also think for you are the people closest to you, your family, your friends, and your followers. Not only may a poor decision impact you, but the trickling effect of that decision could also be expansive and impact many people.

This can be seen in the lives of huge dictators such as Hitler. Hitler felt that he was essential for the masses of people afflicted by the problems of the past, which he determined were the problems of the present. High inflation was one problem, and the other problem was a total annihilation of people unlike him. He manipulated others to see a black hat of leadership that has been a breaking point for the world and human society. Germans still reap the repercussions of Hitler's leadership and in their hearts and minds they are making huge strides to make the world a better place.

Give your full attention to whatever the moment presents. Completely accept what is right now and tend to that.

Controlling others is manipulation, while controlling yourself helps you face your problems head-on.

Just realizing that you may have a weakness is your first step to enlightenment. Then and only then, you can catch yourself right before you take an action and bow out gracefully in the moment. You learn to move on to the next current moment and make the right decision because you now developed a heightened self-awareness.

Send out love and compassion to everyone you know and those that you meet. Do not hold any grudges. Just be love and people will respond with love back.

Conclusion

Use hope, resilience, and optimism to help you stay in the moment. Remember that hope keeps you going in the right direction because it helps you focus on the future, but hope alone is not a strategy. Create a strategy for success in your life and you will achieve it!

Animals give us tremendous joy. Animals love unconditionally and you should too.

Breathe when you find yourself wound up in stress, close your eyes, breathe four counts in, hold for four counts, exhale for four counts, and do not inhale for four counts. Repeat a few times and this will calm your nervous system. Then breathe normally. You are changing your neurology and attracting love in your life.

The joy of living in the moment is an awakening, an enlightenment, and an essence of being that sets you apart from ordinary people that live their life like a candle in the wind.

Hope, resilience, and optimism, coupled with thinking more positive, and less negatively, can bring momentary happiness.

Mindsense creates an aura of joy, an ease of being, and lightness in everything you do. Leave your wake behind you where it belongs. We want to take our jobs and our careers seriously but take our livelihood lightly by living in the moment.

***

CHAPTER 4

Moments
of Conscientiousness

The way to get started is to quit talking and begin doing
—Walt Disney

Life is about risking everything for a dream no one can see but you

—Ray Lewis

Mindsense strategies for avoiding missing out on the present moment are explored in this chapter. Many people are beginning to adapt to mindsense. One woman mentioned to me, "I am looking for an easy going and good-natured man to share beautiful moments in life." She captures the essence of mindsense.

Conscientiousness places you in a state of cognitive ease, or thinking easier, doing something in the moment that puts you in a good mood. Daniel Kahneman, a Nobel Prize winner in economics, wrote a great book titled *Thinking, Fast and Slow*. Dan came up with several categories that lead to this type of thinking. He found four categories that initiate improving the moments in your life.

1. Repeated experience (given that the experience is a good one)
2. Clear display (seeing what you are expected to see)
3. Primed idea (an idea that you own and create in your mind)
4. Good mood (feeling happy in the moment)

Dan found that these states of being led to living in ease, peace, enlightened, and in essence. The reason why these four states help you to live in the moment is because they cause you to feel familiar with what you are doing, feel true for the task or the action (even if it is just relaxing), feel good about your life and your accomplishments, and, most importantly, you feel effortless. You sort of feel like you are in *FLOW*. When you are in flow, you simply revel in the moment.

Psychologists introduced transcendental meditation to college students in textbooks. Many people realize the value of meditation, but some people do not find the time to practice it.

To sit in silence draws upon your inner ability to reason with the outer world. Silence places the ego on hold. We have an endless narrative going on in our mind that may be negative and cause doubt. Doubt is our enemy. We must transcend our thoughts to be positive and visualize a positive future.

Meditation can help you relax and help you connect with the universal power. Without realizing it, each of us practice meditation in some way throughout the day as you breathe easier and more natural.

Naptime in kindergarten was taught at an early age, and the Latin countries call siesta a restful time in the day.

Think of a child growing, every cell in the body is developing. Attempt to go back to this childhood feeling through mediation and relaxation. Living in the present moment makes you feel encouraged, innovative, and creative.

You need to wonder, dream, create, and expand your options to transcend yourself to special places that you love to visit. Your life becomes free of time, and you are beginning to live in the present moment. When stressed, think of happy thoughts, picture yourself at the beach or in the mountains.

The lack of a Mindsense strategy will provide you with a loss of the present moment. As Dan Kahneman mentioned in his thinking hard versus thinking soft idea. Think soft and you may be able to meditate and feel OK, be OK, and think that you are OK just like that child that has every cell of energy growing inside them.

From daydreaming to meditation to deep sleep. We have our day-to-day unconsciousness and our deep sleep unconsciousness. Day dreaming or meditating can be your day-to-day unconsciousness. Sleep is important and we all need it to rejuvenate. We actually grow during sleep as growth hormone is released during our sleep. We also work out conflicts that are in our conscious mind through our subconscious dreams and we process our problems.

One way to enhance your enlightenment is to program yourself before sleep. Try not to watch things that are too dramatic. Set the mood for sleep by relaxing.

Right before you fall asleep you are about to leave the conscious and go into the unconscious world of the universe. The cosmos opens up to your personal intention. Speak to yourself about your intentions.

Deep within the heart and soul of the universe lies the ability to manifest anything you want. You must be confident and have patience and faith because what you want may not manifest itself immediately. Attempt to see your success in the future before you retire for the evening. The mind reaches the boundaries of the universe when you are sleeping.

It takes both intention and direction to accomplish what you want. Many times, we do not ask for what we actually need but we do ask for what we want or desire. The universe does care, and the universe does not deliver immediately but it certainly works in your favor. You must have faith. Faith in the process of manifestation for your desires to come into fruition.

Jen Sincero, author of *You Are a Badass*, offers a refreshingly entertaining guide to reshaping your mindset and your life:

- *Identify and change the self-sabotaging beliefs and behaviors that stop you from getting what you want.*
- *Shift your energy and attract what you desire.*
- *Create a life you totally love. And start creating it NOW.*
- *Make some damn money already. The kind you've never made before.*

The key is to understand how to blast past what's holding you back, make some serious changes, and start living the kind of life that once seemed impossible.

As Henry David Thoreau once said, "Live the Life that You Once Imagined!" This saying is used in the context of pursuing one's dreams with confidence and determination.

Vignette—Joyce's Story of Enlightenment

Joyce was working at a company making $100,000 a year. The company decided to downsize and the house in which she was renting was being sold. Without a job and facing despair she was lost, and she felt despondent. She was unsure of her future and her past was relentlessly haunting her. She went to Narcotics Anonymous meetings to talk about her struggles and was without hope. Her sister encouraged her to hang on and that some way somehow she will survive. She found a garage for rent for $1,500 and she moved some of her stuff there and kept other stuff with friends. There was supposed to be a door on the side of the garage for entry and exiting, but that was not put in.

When the garage door closed, her and her son felt as if the world shut down on them, close to phobic, and encaged. She prayed really hard and found herself at the end of her rope; instead of giving in to her feelings of failure, she tied a knot at the end of her rope of hope and held on tightly, but she still struggled profusely. No furniture, nowhere to live, no help from anyone and trying to keep her sanity. The neighborhood was shady, and she tried to keep her son secure and safe. She prayed that her and her son would survive.

Having a son in high school, with no job, no place to live, and having to store her furniture at various places with friends all stressed her; her stuff was in several basements which added more stress. After hitting bottom and praying profusely with hope and staying clean (a term used to be pure and stay away from controlled substances such as narcotics), she got a call from a friend that just happened to have an apartment for her because someone decided not to take it. She took her stuff, which was not much, and left the garage immediately, did not even pay the lady that rented the garage to her because she only used it for a few days. She took her furniture from the various places and moved on as she apologized to the garage owner and left to live somewhere else. Her friend let her stay in the apartment for free to help her get back on her feet again. She quickly moved her stuff into the apartment and began again with hope and clarity of perspective. A few months later, her sister gave her the keys to a place in Florida and she found a job in which she helps people find work and develops their self-esteem along with their resumes. Joyce was strong enough to not let her past failures endure while keeping the exhausting picture of a negative future at bay. She persevered by living in the moment and thriving with gratitude and resilience.

Joyce survived and is now an example of true triumph through the despair and loss of her livelihood. Joyce developed *mindsense* and lives in the moment with gratitude, resilience, and self-worth. Her son is also thriving. Joyce is an example of manifestation in practice, and she now helps others manifest what they want to accomplish in life. She wears a bracelet that says, "Keep Swimming," a line from the Disney movie *Nemo*.

***

What happened to Joyce could happen to anyone. Joyce focused on the five tenets of Dr. Michael Provitera's book titled *Mastering Self-Motivation*, published by Business Expert Press in 2012:

- **Thrive on Challenging Tasks—Manifest things into your life by setting the precedent for them to come to you.**
- **Have Hope—Linking positive thoughts and self-talk with current and future performance.**
- **Mastering Self-Motivation—Ensure that you are in the moment doing everything you can without worry.**
- **Putting in the Necessary Effort—Everything you touch, do it with all your might.**
- **Being Resilient—Fall forward when mistakes happen and take the lesson as a guide and a necessary step in your progress and growth.**

The key is creating a sense of safety, improving your well-being, and overcoming anxiety of the future.

Understanding mindsense proves beneficial in your personal life because you are better equipped in the present moment to adjust and accept what happens. Practicing mindsense reduces anxiety because when you live in the moment, you reduce the fear of the unknown.

Using mindsense reduces your self-criticism of yourself. By feeling good about yourself, chemical changes take place in your brain and relieves the pressure placed upon yourself. You then have more energy to succeed in the current moment.

Learn from your failures and do not be so critical of mistakes because for every failure is a lesson that improves your performance going forward and better equips you for the future. Let go of any negative self-talk that you may draw upon and be kinder to yourself.

You can also program what you dream. You may even have a vision in a dream. Right before you sleep, try to think about things that matter most to you and the things that you want to manifest into your life. While ready for sleep, attempt to have a pillow that keeps your body as flat as possible. A trick by Neville Goddard, a great enlightener and author, argues that if you say to yourself, as you close your eyes, "I am sleepy, I am so sleepy, so very sleepy," after a while you feel a desire not to move and you feel ready to rest well.

Assume the feeling of what you want and manifest it into reality. Feeling as if you already have what you want will be better in a relaxed state. Imagine what you want in a picture form of what you desire to achieve in life. Believe that you will receive it. The passive state and the feeling of actually having what you want make it happen in your mind. Think with the end in mind. See yourself ascertaining exactly what you want, and the universe will ascertain it for you.

In sleep, we constantly move between a meditative state and phases of dream state. When awake, we may daydream or remember things from our past as we go from ordinary unconsciousness to a daydreaming and back to unconsciousness.

Some people have trouble sleeping. Cats and dogs do not truly sleep because if a strange noise occurs, they automatically wake up. Ordinary unconsciousness is where you are connected to your emotional well-being, your reactions to past events, and your current and future desires are all bunched together.

It is absolutely normal to ponder things from the past or wish things for the future. Anyone, right now, in your company, is so lucky with you.

Do not let people annoy you or take up space in your mind. In this state of mind, your ego is winning over your thought patterns and controlling your every emotion, your memory, your behavior, and your actions. The ego wants you to think that you did something wrong, and you could have handled something better. The ego wants to keep you from failing and the ego wants you to stay safe, protecting itself and not you. Your ego is overpowering.

The ego is a continuous low level of unease that makes you uneasy, discontent, bored, and nervous. Moderation is needed in everything you do because if you overdo any one thing, your ego begins to consume you until you try to let it stop controlling you.

The best indicator of your level of consciousness is how you deal with life's challenges when they enter your life.

Seeking prosperity, happiness, and peace of mind is what mindsense is all about. You begin to have an enlightened life and living with an essence that makes you stand out among others.

People are always wanting more. More money, more land, more toys, more cars, motorcycles, boats, etc. While it is good to manifest things into your life, you must do it with purpose. Imagination works wonders but you do not want to overdo it.

Neville Goddard lectures on how imagination fulfills itself. Goddard believes that imagination creates reality and fulfills itself in what your life becomes. To be enlightened, Goddard argues that until imagination becomes part of your normal, natural thought, you will not act consciously as if you already have it. Goddard says:

> **When you know this [imagination] presence it will not matter if you started life behind the eight-ball, or in a place as a poor child, or a rich child, you would realize that life is always externalizing what you are imagining**—Neville Goddard (Cool Wisdom Books)

Think from the state desired. Be already there in your mind. Some people call this constructive discontent, and as Earl Nightingale calls it, moving forward in discontent. Goal setting due to discontent is sort of programmed in some people and this is the unseen enemy of enlightenment. With mindsense, you understand how the mind functions and you start making headway because you begin to realize the energy of the subconscious mind. Use discipline and desire to win what you want in life.

James Doty, the author of a new book called *Mind Magic*, and his earlier book titled *Into the Magic Shop*, says, in a YouTube video titled "The Universe Doesn't Give a F*ck About You!"

Doty offers a neuroscientific perspective by explaining how to maximize manifestation. He also argues that "The teacher comes when the student is ready."

If you do not use the universal powers that are always available to you, the universe cannot help you and it does not care about you. If you do, you have a better chance to achieve greatness.

Like Stephen Covey, in his book, *The 7 Habits of Highly Effective People*, said, begin with the end in mind.

Neville Goddard also said thinking from the end is the beginning of all miracles.

James Allen, in his book *As a Man Thinketh*, argues that the body is the servant of the mind. The body is a delicate instrument, which responds readily to the thoughts by which it is impressed, and habits of thought will produce their own effects, good or bad, upon it.

The old west was riddled with gunman that had low self-esteem and some had to tell people what their names were and what they had done in the past. Cowboys coming into a town weather-drawn, lonely, uneasy, and restless would want to have some fun. The undercurrent of this constant unease of the cowboy started long before the old west. This became an underpinning identification of the cowboy of the old west. Just like all people and culture, there lie good and bad folks.

In order to offset this graylike view of the cowboy, a few cowboys got together and created the cowboy code of ethics. Here are a few of the cowboy principles:

The cowboy must never shoot first, never hit a smaller man, or take unfair advantage of someone.

The cowboy must never go back on his word, or a trust confided in him with another person or companion.

The cowboy must always tell the truth.

The cowboy must be gentle with children, the elderly, and animals.

The cowboy must not advocate or possess racially or religiously intolerant ideas.

He must help people in distress.

These principles are a good code of ethics for anyone to follow.

My father always told me that "familiarity breeds contempt." He told me that once a person gets to know you or finds out what you own, they may be in contempt to feel a sense of jealousy, envy, or dislike toward you.

When you resist the present moment as your only time in your life that you ever actually have, you forget not only where you came from but also where you are going.

Be happy with what you have and praise people that have more without contempt or jealousy. The saying, "Keeping Up with the Joneses, " is a competition that neighbors have had for centuries. May have even led the fighting between the Hatfields and the McCoys, in the old west.

Freud recognized this undercurrent of unease when comparing yourself to others as the survival mind and the adventure mind. If you waste your current moment on the survival mind, you focus your attention (both purposefully and automatically) toward the future in order to achieve desired results in the moment. You scan the dangers and promote the feeling of being in control of the future.

The survival mind functioning draws on associating present cues with past experience and applying prior solutions to present circumstances. Sometimes we can waste a great deal of time in the present moment because we associate with past experience and apply prior solutions to present circumstances. However, we are citing our failed choices or our fatal flaws and this is a total waste of the current moment.

The Adventure Mind is where people are absorbed in living fully for the moment. The guiding principle here is that you stay in the adventure mind and follow your interest in the present moment. As Dan Kahneman mentioned earlier, "Slow Think" will guide you if you just let it take its course.

Dan demonstrates that the vast majority of people trust their beliefs over evidence to the contrary. He called this "Fast Think" in which we judge everything by our values, our assumption, our beliefs, and our expectations.

Dan came up with some ways to use "Going with the Flow," and his main idea is a differentiation between two modes of thought: one being thinking fast, instinctive and emotional; the other thinking slower, more deliberative, and more logical. Here are some examples of when we use "Slow Think."

- Flow comes from when you are engaged in an effortless task
- When you are in a good mood because in the moment you thought of a happy episode in your life
- When you score low on a depression test
- When you are a knowledgeable novice on a topic or task and not a true expert
- When you score high on a scale of faith in intuition
- When you are (or are made to feel) powerful

This topic is important to mindsense because some people just have to know how they feel and do not need to know of some poll or some empirical study to influence them to think a certain way or the right way to act.

Going with the flow is what Freud called the Adventure Mind. It sounds like world travel, but it actually describes a positive mental functioning in the present moment. Here, you are absorbed in living fully for the moment.

The guiding principle of the Adventure Mind is to follow your own interest in the present moment, wherever it goes, and do not get bogged down from your past experiences or future plans. Simply feel good about going into the new and take this in stride in the present moment.

Three things that impact a person's VABES (Values, Assumptions, Beliefs, and Expectations of how they feel the world is and how the world should be), according to Jim Clawson:

- Consciousness—a behavior in which you are in a state of being awake and aware of your surroundings. Visible behavior.
- Semiconsciousness behavior or in some cases partially conscious behavior because you are only somewhat awake and able to understand what is happening around you. You may feel a sixth sense in this state, using all your senses.

- Unconsciousness behavior is where you are uniformed or un-aware. These are your VABES, and they are part of your beauty, both inside and out; maybe part of you is being unconscious of it, but much of your behavior comes from here.

Our ego can impact our unconsciousness and impact the consciousness without you realizing it.

The key is to live in the moment and always be attempting to determine how you feel by monitoring your thoughts and your self-talk.

We are controlled by our ego and our ego wants us to stay in consciousness and succeed, or, in some cases, our ego wants to protect us from making a fool of ourselves or failing. You must be aware of how little control you have over this process. Self-awareness is key here, and mindsense warns us that there is not a secret formula to becoming enlightened and having an essence about yourself.

Mindsense simply warns you to keep on moving toward your best self and not let your past or current stress get in the way of your happiness.

VABEs, as Jim mentions, stand for:

Values that you collected growing up until now,
Assumptions you developed over your lifetime,
Beliefs that you or others impressed on you, and
Expectations about what you expect the world to be like.

These VABEs of how you feel the world is and how it should be impact your present moment. This is absolutely profound knowledge that a person must understand about oneself and attempt to learn other people's VABES when necessary.

Jim found that over 95 percent of our actions and behavior come from our unconscious and semiconscious VABEs.

Observe the many ways that your mind is triggered from a past consequence or trauma that you experienced. It just pops up. This unease or discontent is real, and, in many cases, tension arises within you through your critical self and unnecessary judgment of the past.

An example of this from the movie *Goodwill Hunting* shows how the scars of childhood could impact an adult's life, even if that adult is very intelligent. You may be resisting what is in front of you and denying the current moment due to a past memory or a future concern.

Sometimes you cannot see where you are going from where you are currently sitting. Mindsense helps you become aware of this and helps you begin to feel OK with yourself while you are alone. It is called strategic silence; you see a brighter future and, you tell no one until you show up there. Strategic silence looks at the glass half full all the time. The glass half empty is your past coming back to haunt your present moment.

As a thought pops into your mind from your past or your subconscious mind leaking into your consciousness, shine light on it, smile, accept it; once you become conscious of it then it no longer is a burden to you. This may take time, especially if you have been this way for a long time. Just catch it and you may be able to stop the thought before it gets worse. Your heightened self-awareness is resolving your internal conflict.

VABEs are developed over time from your childhood, your upbringing, and your current circumstance.

Shakespeare once said, "It is better to have love and lose it, then to never have love at all." Some people never find love, and this is truly sad for them.

Perhaps Shakespeare wrote *Romeo and Juliet* for people that either have love or have lost it. His intention is love if you can.

According to data from 2023 from Quora, a frequently used Internet site, it is more common for people to have been in at least one romantic relationship than to have never been in a relationship. Surveys indicate that around 10 percent to 20 percent of adults report having never been in a committed romantic relationship.

It is a fact that some people do not find love in the modern society we live. For now, live in the moment and love yourself. By loving yourself, you become more attractive to your partner.

While your unconsciousness may be your nemesis to some extent, it can be controlled with active visualizations and reprogramming your mind. First, you must realize that it exists. Buried thoughts can be a powerful tool to help you become more enlightened. The semiconscious or unconscious mind is very powerful in controlling not only the way you think on a momentary basis but also helps you control your behavior in many situations throughout the day. Being aware of your thoughts will help you to deal with your semiconscious or unconscious mind effectively.

Day dreaming and thinking in the moment is a pondering mode, and this is preprogrammed by your ordinary unconsciousness, and this may not be as easy to detect because it comes natural to us as we draw on a reminder of our past. Make it a habit to monitor your thoughts as they arise and honor them, no matter if they are negative or positive. Positivity is encouraged, while negative thoughts need to be reprogrammed.

Your thoughts are usually connected in something from your past that is intruding on your present moment. Do not judge your ordinary unconsciousness; just be aware of it.

Talking out your feelings instead of keeping them bottled up inside of you is also very helpful. In the movie *Pretty Woman*, Richard Gere states in a line that it took him 10 years of therapy for him to be able to say, "I hate my father."

Do not get angry at your thought process because then you are letting your unconscious mind win and take over your current moment. Mindsense grasps the moment and understands that a certain situation may have nothing to do with you now and, therefore, it is not internalized as a problem. When you focus on the problems that you have or perceive to be happening to you, you create more problems for yourself. When you focus on solutions to the real or even the perceived problems happening to you, you see more opportunities to embrace and help yourself thrive.

Managing unhappiness. It is up to you to decide how happy you want to be. No one can make you happy. It has to come from deep down inside. Every morning, be happy to be awake and in good health, show gratitude. Then, review your thinking pattern. Are you thinking negatively? If so, it could be a bad dream or modern-day worries. If you feel sad, attempt to change the way you are thinking. Think positive thoughts, if you have a pet, go over to your dog or cat and pet them. Animals tend to cheer people up.

If you carry resentment of any kind, it will eat away at you. No matter what you resent, it is your past and not your present moment right now. If you truly do have trouble in your life, you will have to address this situation in the present moment. Once you have addressed the problem, move on to enjoying the next moment. Life is short and there is no replay button.

Your mind is like a garden, and you have to tend to the weeds. Your negative and past thoughts are weeds. Think of growing a tiger lily. The tiger lily is often associated with wealth, prosperity, and good luck in the Chinese culture. In the language of flowers, it is said to represent pride, prosperity, and hardiness. In the language of mindsense, it is your new path, and it is your true north.

Conclusion

Being conscientious is a trait that people should have. A very important concept for mindsense is to help people live with passion and enlightenment. Knowing your own VABES will help you let go of the past. You can learn a lesson from the past and plan on using the echoes of knowledge gained from the past, but you cannot change it.

Try to feel your semiconscious beliefs when they occur and move them to your consciousness. Jim Clawson, the emeritus professor of leadership and organizational behavior at the Darden School of Business, at the University of Virginia, discovered VABEs for a good reason in his Level Three Leadership Model. Knowing your VABES lets you live with a clarity of purpose, clarity of a vision that you want to pursue, and a moral compass to keep you on track.

Manage your own moments because other people have their own problems managing their own emotions.

There are so many things to resent in our life. The time we waste on resentment takes away from your current moment. Live for right now in this moment. You are worthy and entitled to every moment.

***

CHAPTER 5

Being Present in the Moment

Speak less, maintain an air of seriousness, focus on developing your mind (while not neglecting your body), and start practicing dignity and discipline

—Epictetus, Greek Philosopher

The present moment is a gift; do not take it for granted. Thoughts badger us as we drive, disturb us when we are bored, interfere with us when we watch something on television. Thoughts are not what you think they are.

Zen teaches us to just be. When no thought appears then you are in the present moment for at least the time being. With no thoughts coming into your mind, you are alert and happy. This is why it is important to overcome distraction.

Think of working in spurts of time so that your moment is not camouflaged with past thoughts or future expectations. Use the "Pandora method" of working for 25 minutes, then breaking. The method is actually called the Pomodoro technique. "Pomodoro" is Italian for "tomato," and the method involves setting a timer for 25 minutes of focused work followed by a 5-minute break, often using a kitchen timer shaped like a tomato. Interesting enough, you can accomplish a great deal using this method. The key is when you break, really break and stretch, walk, or meditate. Sure, this is a time to answer emails or texts but do it in a relaxed mode. Then return to your task at hand.

People tend to put things out of their mind saying that they do not care about a person or thing. Or they are overoccupied with their present stress. We have been given intellectual qualities that no other form or species have, and this does not mean that you need to get a college degree or even a high school degree to tap into this intelligence.

Using your perception, your will, your reason, your imagination, your memory, and your intuition is all you need to possess the infinite power of manifestation. Power that is derived from the universe.

Epictetus was a Greek philosopher and Stoic who developed the Stoic philosophies of earlier thinkers which help us stay in the moment as we create the world in which we live. Some of his quotes are worth noting.

- "No man is free who is not master of himself."
- "Wealth consists not in having great possessions, but in having few wants."
- "Circumstances don't make the man, they only reveal him to himself."
- "In prosperity it is very easy to find a friend; but in adversity it is the most difficult of all things."

Epictetus's teachings emphasize self-mastery, virtue, and living a good life. He believed that people should focus on improving their reason and making good choices, rather than being concerned about what others think. He also believed that true freedom comes from within, through self-discipline and control over desires.

Epictetus had great insights into being more self-aware in the moment. He helped people become more self-aware.

- We must think of the way that we talk to ourselves and the story we create out of any experience to ensure the narrative is positive.
- Learn how to recognize when you distort reality so that you can be kinder and more compassionate to yourself.
- You can choose your own path of action, but not others because we are not able to control everything. Losing our control on our life, sets us free.
- Being surrounded by negative people can lead you to have a very pessimistic view of the world. Be less pessimistic and more optimistic.

This is how advertising works. Thoughts found in advertisements are placed in your subconscious and lay dormant in your mind, but this thought controls your behavior. We buy things or do things without knowing why. This is based on our own inductive reasoning, which is any of the various methods of reasoning in which broad generalizations or principles are derived from our observations.

In other circumstances, we step back and ponder a choice. This is our deductive reasoning, which is the process of drawing valid inferences. An inference is valid if its conclusion follows logically from its premise, meaning that it is impossible for the premises to be true and the conclusion to be false. Therefore, if you set aside your inductive reasoning, your imaginative thoughts go directly to your subconscious mind in which it is stored and retrieved without you even knowing. This is why advertising attempts to fascinate us.

Advertising gets us to nod in agreement or shock us into some type of action or behavior. The worst and best commercials are remembered. Many things that you see or hear are stored in your subconscious. This is important because the conscious mind can dictate what is going into the subconscious mind by being aware of your thoughts and actions without judging them.

Being conscious is being cool, calm, and collected, and when conscious sinks below a certain level of enlightenment, thoughts rush in like a tsunami. You say to yourself, that is not like me, something else went wrong such as lack of sleep or lack of protein.

Victor Frankl, a Holocaust survivor, discovered logotherapy that describes a search for life's meaning as the central human motivational force. He said that regardless of the intellectual or physical abuse that a person can be subjected to, in his case it was during his captured time of torture during the Holocaust, no one can cause you to think something that you do not want to think.

The essence of who you are cannot be shattered by people, places, or things. When you develop this inside-out versus outside-in approach to life, your thoughts are omnipresent. Your thinking becomes an enormous power because your thoughts are the most pertinent energy. As Earl Nightingale said, *you become what you think about.*

You start from your thought to the idea to what you desire or want to have. Do not work from the outside-in because the universe does not care about what you think, it only nurtures what you think once you think it: good or bad.

A commercial once noted that *The Mind Is a Terrible Thing to Waste*. It appealed to drug addicts. Coming out of a movement by Nancy Reagan, a former U.S. president's wife, who was a huge proponent of "Say No to Drugs." Nancy made a lasting impression just like advertisements do, but the first lady's message was doomed because she was planting the seed of, "You can never get enough of what you do not want." Her catchphrase did not work because individuals subject to Drug Awareness Resistance Education (DARE) remain just as likely to use drugs as those who receive no anti-drug messages. A better approach would be the *Reflected Best Self Exercise*, which only focuses on strengths and building upon them without the negative connotation.

Unfortunately, the mental noise in our mind is relentless. We cannot get enough of what we do not want. The more we want it, the more the thought rears its ugly clutch on us. We must accept this, acknowledge it, and say, "There I go again," and know that in time the thought will pass. Some thoughts may linger longer but acknowledging them will help them dissipate.

You come into this world alone and you will leave alone, and people also need to leave you alone; do not let negative people take up space in your mind.

Remember that stillness as well as relaxation is your goal in life, and you do not need to be disrupted with thoughts of others taking over your space in your mind. You cannot go back in time in reality, but your mind has a strong tendency to do so. Cherish the good memories and smile. Don't go back in time; stay present.

Zen masters teach that surprise is always lurking. They feel that if you are not ready for surprise then you are not ready to be enlightened.

Vignette—The Miracle of Mindfulness by Thich Nhat Hanh

To set up mindfulness, figure out a way to remind yourself at the moment of waking that this day is your day of mindfulness. This is your day. While lying in bed, begin slowly to follow your breath. Take slow, long, and conscious breaths. Then slowly rise from bed (instead of turning out all at once as usual), nourishing mindfulness by every motion. Once up, do all your morning activities in a calm and relaxing way, each movement done in mindfulness. Every moment should be done calmly, and maintain a half smile.

***

The idea offered by Hanh can be followed in anything you do. Just be wherever you are and enjoy it.

To be in the current moment, take care of yourself, not only for yourself but also for your loved ones that want you to be around as long as possible. The alcoholic destroys not only oneself but the whole family that sees him or her deteriorate. This action has a trickledown effect on the family.

Make the current moment be deeply rooted within yourself and your mind. Get off the wild rapids of the current thought patterns that cause anxiety and depression.

My father always said, "Time heals all wounds, Son." I remember those words when I hit bottom in relationships and life. Have a presence of inner peace, an inner energy field that portrays the way for happiness within yourself. The great Bruce Lee said the punch comes from within. Inner energy. Develop this in your mind and thoughts.

The new is something worth getting used to. In my *Reflected Best Self Exercise* I often ask people to create a visual that they can relate to in a successful way. Make a vision board by letting your mind think in images. Images of the things and experiences that you want to manifest are hugely powerful because your mind sends those images to the universe. The universe is your to source of energy which begins the process of attracting more of what you want toward you. The universe is like a magnet that looks at you as the center of the universe. Watts says it best as he reveals the secret of life:

> *'Tatvamasi*.' You are it. You are everything that is going on. In other words, you are in a particular place at which the whole universe is focused. And every one of us is an aperture through*

---

*A word from Hindu philosophy (could be spelled Tat Tvam Asi). Tat refers to all existence or ultimate reality. Tvam means you, referring to the individual self. Asi means are, signifying the identity or unity between the individual self and the ultimate reality.

which this entire cosmos is watching itself. Of course, there are lots of these apertures because the system arranges itself so that it is not to be narrow-minded and prejudice. So, it looks at itself at ever so many points of view. And each one of us, therefore, is really, as we feel ourselves to be, the center of the universe. And that would be true if we were living on the planet earth or a planet in some other galaxy altogether.

Waiting for something new to come into your life is an exceptional time riddled with both hope and doubt. The enlightened person feels OK with this knowing that something good will show up soon or in the near future. If it takes longer, the enlightened person still knows that it will come.

Enjoying the present moment is a sense of waiting and relaxing with yourself. When you wait, wait in good spirit, realize the good things that you have and celebrate them in your mind. Ann Provitera called this *"peace of mind."* It is a valuable state of presence that only the enlightened mind has mastered. Relax with yourself while you wait yet be totally aware of your presence.

Waiting requires your readiness for the unknown. A person may come into your life, the phone could ring with a job offer, a book acceptance, a program acceptance, or just a phone call from someone that you miss and have been thinking about. Always be ready for the unknown and know that something could happen at any moment and be absolutely aware when it occurs. While waiting, be still, concentrate on your presence.

All of your attention has to be in the present moment, or you will miss it. Act only in the present moment, be aware of your surroundings, plan, and make decisions in the present moment.

Meditation or day dreaming is a natural stillness of your present moment. We learn from Zen that the experience of awakening or what we know in the state as enlightenment is the true nature of reality. Zen calls this to be a second of realization in a superpower that comes to those willing and ready to accept it. Zen masters say that you can learn Zen in 3 seconds or 30 years. Failures or debilitating thoughts of our past and losses may fog the present moment. We must realize that the mind will recall the episodes in the present moment until your mind no longer needs to do so. People attempt to blur the thoughts with drugs or alcohol, but that only places a

Band-Aid on the problem and does not heal it. When the time comes when you will no longer think of the debilitating thoughts of the past, which are very real, mind you, it is then that you have a reason to be grateful. When this pivotal point comes to you it gives you a chance to feel enlightened.

In the book *Don Quixote*, Miguel de Cervantes speaks of an eagle passing over him while walking with a student, on a trail, and he told the student that means that they have been enlightened because the eagle chose them as their acknowledgment of a higher spirit.

You have to experience life and put down the personal baggage of problems, things of the past or things that you feel negatively about. You cannot give up the forest for the trees. The trees make the forest, and the forest would be bare without them. Your total presence in the current moment is necessary for your enlightenment.

The mind sponges off of the cerebral cortex of the brain which is the brain's outermost layer. This area of the brain is responsible for memory, thinking, learning, reasoning, and problem-solving. This is where you store all your experiences in your life. The mind does not care to create a beautiful life for you; it basically works off what you stored there. The cortex of the brain exists as a storage facility of all the good and bad things that happened to you. The mind can neither recognize nor create beauty.

The moment that you do not recall the baggage of your past, you are free from your mind controlling your life and your behavior. At that time, your thoughts provide a feeling of enlightenment.

The conscious self, therefore, is not afraid of the unknown. Embrace the unknown. Do not be afraid to start over again, you may like your new story better than the last one.

To be conscious you must feel your surroundings fully. Use all five senses. Just being alive is consciousness. We all know stories of people dying quickly and peacefully while reading or resting. The heart just stops. Life itself and consciousness are one and the same. Your presence, whether you are bored or happy, silent or moving around, you are very conscious of yourself and you are as present as you will ever be.

People may not care about your consciousness because they only care about themselves. This is a narcissistic attitude that many people have. Be aware of it and do not look for others to make your present moment of happiness, make your "self" happy for being alive and grateful for every moment.

You will often refer to your most recent past because it is at the top of the totem pole of your thought process. Lower on the totem pole of your past is where the secrets to your consciousness exist. You must learn to let go and focus on the current moment. Bored or happy, it is your moment for now and the only one you ever have. The past thoughts cannot survive in the current moment unless you let them.

The past pain and suffering is gone now. While enlightened, the past is a fog that has drifted. James Dean, the famous actor that died early in life, once said, *"Dream as if you will live forever, and live as you will die today."* According to this logic you already beat your past and you survived another day.

Find the present moment you own and share it with someone. Never let the past of the unpleasant time spent with another person ruin your feeling of superiority and wholeness. Recognize the presence of enlightenment. Try to attract enlightened people in your life.

You can manifest this by just being yourself in the moment and relaxing. Think of nothing but the present moment. Your ego will convince you that your life could always be better.

Nothing good happens after midnight unless you create it with the people you care about. Darkness is a time to sleep, not creep. Zen masters say when you eat, eat, and when you sleep, sleep. Stay in the moment at these special times of your life.

Join people that feel the same, think the same, and care about similar interests. The more people enlightened in your life, the merrier you will be. When people you care about are around you, things you do feel better. Make and cherish memories with enlightened people. A positive state of presence exists when like minds are together celebrating their own self-worth with others.

Many times, nothing needs to be said, a strong energy emulates the room because a collective energy offers a sense of oneness. Surrounding yourself with like minds frees up negative energy and bad energy. You are building a zone of indifference in which you act without a great deal of effort or thought.

Conclusion

Anything can happen in the present moment. Your presence is all you need in the moment. You are awake when you act in the direction of your dreams.

We see advertisements of lifestyles and material things that we wish to have. Advertising sometimes distorts our viewpoint the same way that social media provides false narratives of other people's success and fame, leaving us feeling inadequate. Reversing these feelings of lack offers you a sense of presence and enlightenment.

Hypnosis and affirmations are powerful because the right seeds in your mind will grow in your subconscious, where more happens than you actually know in your mind.

Animals have a fascinating existence. Kittens are so playful. They swipe at you with no nails out on their paws. They bounce off your forehead. When a cat is ready to pounce on a mouse, it gets ready and focuses on only that event. Cats know how to live in the moment. Have the focus of a cat and by being mindful of your actions and behavior.

When someone does not want to be in your company or wants to be somewhere else than with you, that is their problem, not yours. They own the problem. Let them go do what they want because only they can control their moments while you control yours.

***

CHAPTER 6

Moments in the Universe

If you are not fired up with enthusiasm, you will be fired without enthusiasm

—*Vince Lombardi*

It is important that you understand that the present moment is your pathway for enlightenment. Not every moment can be your best moment. There will be times that you are just sitting, just planning, or just wishing.

The universe is so vast and phenomenal that you are just another part of it while you are alive. Your soul is the center of the universe, your heart is the temple in which you exist, and your brain is the mechanism to get you through life. All this is connected to the vast universe.

Making decisions based on what you want to attract into your life, then using visualization, and discipline by doing this often and in the proper manner, gets you to look beyond your thoughts. Focus on Earl Nightingale's great idea:

> **Have a great attitude, create, monitor, and renew your goals, and keep raising the bar on your potential, even if it is a slight raise.**

If a thought seems to be fleeting, drop it. As Sylvester Stallone, the movie actor, once said, "drop your thought like a bad habit if it is getting in the way of your progress." Think inside-out. Try to work from the end of what you want to the present moment. The reason for this is that there is this universal energy running through us and if you decide what you want and act as if you already have it, your mind does not know the difference of having it or not. You raise the frequency just like you would raise the thermostat to make your home warmer. As you raise your frequency, you act like the person that you want to become.

The inner neocortex of the brain is storing these thoughts and feeding them to the frontal limbic part of your brain. The stronger and longer the impression made on your brain from that thought, the more power the neocortex has over your thought process. You can fight it, but just let it roll until it fades like all the other thoughts that have faded in your life.

Life is too short to limit yourself to weak attempts to try to diminish your thoughts and your neediness. No one likes someone that is needy. Be strong, be forthright, but try not to ever be needy.

This logic of thoughts that bounce off your mind is related to your scientific makeup. It comes from biology, not psychology. The brain is very expansive. Your brain heals without your intentional control. Just live in the moment and do not try to control your brain. You must replace the thoughts with new ones. A dead cell phone does nothing for you just like an ego that has no one to impress but itself.

Imagine a person with a high ego surrounded by mirrors; it is as if the mindsense is gone and the person is dealing with collective insanity. Do not get stuck on a thought level, acknowledge it, be aware of it, even be frustrated with it, but let it run its course. The ego wants to keep you with that thought attempting to tell you that you failed, you are wrong, you must fight for what you want, call the person, get the job, find the life you lost, and so on. The ego mind is stubborn and does not care about you; it only cares about its presence inside you and how it can control your thoughts and behavior.

A thought is no more than a means to an end and the end is your own personal frustration. The ego is a detraction and abstraction to what really matters. Should you be concerned about your health, the way you look and feel? Yes. Should it be an obsession? No. The ego will make your looks and your outfit an obsession if you let it.

In a part of Florida called St. Augustine, there is a fountain of youth. The myth has it that if you drink from the fountain of youth, then you will stay young forever. Your ego would like to agree with that. It is an old folk tale, but many people drink from it anyway.

Past thoughts provide points that are beyond our control and could be frustrating at times. Let your negative, debilitating, or sad thoughts dissolve over time. They will.

Tapping into the power of the universe is available to everyone. It is like religion: Does a small boy in Tanzania, eastern Africa, have the same ability to draw upon the universal power as someone living in New York City? Yes.

The body is a vessel that got you from birth to now and the one thing that we all agree upon is that we are going to die someday. When you die, the body, the flesh, is still in decay mode, but your soul is what exists beyond death. Tapping into your soul while alive is your freedom to enlightenment.

The soul, like your charisma, is the animated version of you. Feed the soul with love and happiness and this will extend beyond your current outer version of your body. Within your soul is the power of the universe. The connection is real, and the energy is powerful.

Try holding your palms up and feel how you feel the energy of the universe in the palms of your hand right at that moment. Then turn them down and feel how your hands feel at that moment; they may feel less energy from the universe. That is the universal energy that you can tap into because when you attempt to tap the universal powers, the universe sends energy toward you.

Manifestation is the connection of your soul with the universe and transformation is how enlightenment happens. Feel your body from the inside-out as opposed to the outside-in. That is your connection to the universe.

Your soul and mind pervades the body and gives vibrant life to every organ and every cell. Feel it. Feel that you have an aura around you, a zone of indifference.

Similar to your peripheral vision, you can see beyond the frontal aspect of your vision. From a visual standpoint, you can sense someone staring at you even outside your peripheral vision.

Transformational Leadership of the Mind

Transformational leadership is a way your body leads itself through the stages of life. If you look at your hand, it certainly changed a great deal since you were young. Treat your body like a temple. We often look at our own body with a pleasant or an unpleasant feeling. Your body is not your whole being. While alive, you must live your best life. The inner body that carries your soul is an unlimited vessel that lives on forever.

It is important to connect with your inner self as much as possible. Being more consciousness of your inner body. If you feel a bad feeling in your stomach, it may be a sign that something is wrong. Monitoring your inner self leads to higher levels of intuition and discernment.

The higher the vibrational frequency of the inner body the more synchronicity takes place. Thinking of someone and then the phone rings or just knowing something needs to be done before it actually needs to be done is your inner awareness connecting with outside energy. When you act at this level, you are working at a higher frequency.

Other people's jealousy, envy, or negativity cannot affect you now that you are in control of your own destiny.

Now you are on the pathway to think inside-out. At this level of consciousness, greater things happen to you, you tend to attract new circumstances that reflect this higher frequency of both knowledge and intellect.

Attempt to keep your energy within your body as a way of projecting outward, feel as if you are special and that you have a chip on your shoulder. You are magnanimous. People are genuinely attracted to you. This attention will be anchored in the current moment.

Love people unconditionally. It is hard to not hold a grudge when someone hurts you emotionally. Try not to have hate in your heart, do not hold grudges, and forgive those who abandoned you. In many cases, it is not their fault any way. They are caught up in themselves; they are egotistic or narcissistic.

You are probably holding a grudge against someone from an old fling, a sibling, or a partner. This too may be in your neocortex of your brain feeding your behavior. As you search within yourself, you will realize that they did not try to hurt you. They may have made a mistake or wanted to secure their own negative feelings from being exposed.

Focus on your inner well-being. Relax, feel good, and do not expect everything to work out accordingly your plans. Life is just not that simple.

These thoughts of loss will surface, usually at night, or early morning, when you are cold and lonely, sometimes while driving, and probably when something negative occurs in your life. Just observe the emotion and understand it is your brain sending thoughts, feel it fully, acknowledge your thoughts, and accept them. Do not feel sad or wish that the thought did not surface. Do not ask yourself why the thought keeps surfacing. Fully accept this feeling and do not fight it. The uneasiness you feel is a natural tendency of the body to deflect, acknowledge, and help you move on. Do not get drowned in vices that may make you more depressed. You are becoming more aware and more secure in and of yourself. Alan Watts provides a good solid piece on why things do not work out in relationships. Watts argues that you never lost anything; you may have freed yourself from a lingering painful relationship that may have gotten worse. Attempt to address the feelings head-on. Anger, for example, is real; get angry, but watch as you catch yourself getting angry, so you do not get angrier. It dissipates because you became aware of it. That is where enlightenment begins to kick in. Awareness of what you are feeling is how you can put it past you. The same with thinking before you speak and say the wrong thing, catch yourself and practice strategic silence.

In many cases you are creating a problem that does not exist. Say to yourself, "I am feeling a bit angry now." By acknowledging the anger, you realize that you are not anger itself, you simply are feeling the emotion of anger.

Attention is the key to transformational leadership of oneself. If you are let down or feeling a sense of loss, that may be the transformation that you need to see the shift. Something far greater is at work when you are feeling uncomfortable. Life steps in to disrupt that comfortableness. A seed buried in the earth does not remain a seed, it grows under the soil the same way that you transform yourself.

When relationships end, the boss decides terminate you, this may be a sign that you are being prepared for something far better. We see the immediate pain and discomfort, but that is the spark of transformation.

Change implies acceptance, tolerance, and awareness. It is a focused power of your inside-out consciousness that puts you in the driver seat and places your thoughts and feeling in the right place.

Manifesting with resonance and transformation sets you on a path for your true north. It is similar to a light that we see when we close our eyes and meditate or before we go to sleep. That light is our true north and the pathway to true manifestation of universal power. The power of the moment. This light we see when we close our eyes is the source from which consciousness emanates and drives our manifestation.

When Wayne Dyer asked Oprah Winfrey how she became so successful, she said, "I created it;" she was indicating that she manifested her success.

By exercising, you are taking care of the vessel that carries the mind and soul. You build a fitness plateau and then you improve your fitness incrementally. We have a capacity to grow until we die. The biggest problem with age is the psychological aspects of it, not the fact that the body wilts while the mind grows. It is amazing how you have changed over the years.

The mind, if you nurture it, develops, expands, and feeds the aging process with the recognition necessary to keep a high self-esteem and self-efficacy. You become more enlightened in consciousness because your self-esteem and self-efficacy, which is the feeling that you can survive anywhere, anyplace, at any time, gives you the impetus to keep going in life.

After COVID-19, the immune system has been brought to light. People died. The immune system is your combustion engine and ensuring that it is healthy is one of your highest priorities to ensure enlightenment. George Burns, the famous older actor, was asked how he stays in shape, and he said, "I eat sparingly." Food could be your enemy as depicted in the film *The Whale*, which portrays a man eating himself to death in 1 week's time.

Body mass index (BMI) is somewhat elusive, but body fat is not; controlling body fat is challenging but necessary to your well-being. Exercising 1 hour a day adds 3 hours to your life, and sleeping and meditating help your body self-heal.

The *turkey syndrome*, introduced by an author of a Business Expert Press book, presents a common fallacy about the turkey. However, the idea is a fact of reality. Most people in America love Thanksgiving and millions of people eat turkey on Thanksgiving. A turkey is well fed, nurtured, and coddled for 18 months, then the day before Thanksgiving, it gets its head cut off unexpectedly. We all have a turkey syndrome within us and around us, that we may be neglecting or are unaware of that could suddenly happen suddenly. We must look at all aspects of our life to see if we are sleeping well, eating well, resting well and take action on any minor change to our health that we must act upon before it is too late.

Observe how you feel on a regular basis, find your weak spots and weed out the things that can harm you. Annual physicals are necessary. Having a clean bill of health is a virtue.

After taking care of your physical health, enhance your psychic immune system. This helps you fight off the daily stress.

Create a protective positive mental emotional force field that places you in a zone of indifference. When 9/11/2021 took place, it was so terrible but the image of the building falling in our minds and on the news and people diving to their death made it even worse.

When you secure your mental and physical force field, you rule out the negative frequency vibration that is all around you. Living in the moment builds an entire energy field that fights off fear, anger, depression, and stress. This is because the vibration of this negativity is at a much lower frequency than your state of being. Your moments are valid, fruitful, and meaningful and you set up a different sense of reality.

The stuff that bothers others does not impact you any longer because your level of consciousness is above the fray like an eagle soaring above. You no longer let the outside-in approach to life impact you because you increased your level of enlightenment and consciousness.

Breathe often and with intention. Intentional breathing is very important for our health and well-being. Taking deep breaths helps you get acclimated to the day. Under stress, breathing helps tame your central nervous system. Let the breath take your mind and thinking into the body. Saying a mantra as you breathe in and out, helps you focus on relaxing and meditating. Conscious breathing can help you with enlightenment and as the Zen teachings express try to take the middle ground. Do not over focus on one thing and do not try to eliminate the focus on one thing.

Innovation and creativity is tantamount to your enlightenment. The most creative time of your life is right before you wake, right before you sleep, and when you are awakened by a dream.

If you put garbage into your brain, then you will get garbage out with your thoughts. Try to focus on a positive thought. Nice calm and peaceful things. Draw you're your inner strength and fortitude from positive psychology by reflecting on your best self. Focus on your inner energy field and your positive thinking. Become aware of your stillness, feel cozy in bed, revel in the comfort of your pillow and blanket in bed. Stay warm and relax your whole body. This way your mind will be creative and innovative while you sleep. Listen to your inner voice which will guide you.

Make it a habit to check your emotions, check your reactions, and check your inner feelings, this inner type of listening will become your source of thinking with the whole body and not just your mind or gut feelings.

Lean in when around people. The art of listening is a virtue that can give clues to their mind, their thoughts, and their intentions. You can sense when someone is not with you on the same level, when a partner is uncaring or acting like a wallflower. You will feel the intention deep inside of you while listening to them and watching them act. The question is what to do with this knowledge. If you flinch or get angry you will let the person know that you know that you aware of their inner intentions. Funny thing is they may not even be aware of how they are acting but you see right through them to their inner core. Just act like you are listening normally but feel the person's words with your whole body. The energy field of your whole body will give you the clue. Practice strategic silence.

When you listen with your whole body, you leave the person with the feeling that they gave you without showing them how it impacted or affected you. This is hard at first but after trial, error, and habit, you will master it.

The poker face is powerful and is a part of strategic silence. When poker players play cards, the winners only have good cards 12 percent of the time, the other 88 percent they bluff. Become an expert at bluffing.

Bow out gracefully and take the high road when faced with loss of friends, lovers, partners, or jobs. Be very careful not to show your cards and keep the poker face. You will survive to live another day and persevere. Be calm, be cool, be collected. This may take attention away from your thinking and may create a stillness and steadiness space that enables you to truly listen without the mind and thoughts interfering.

You cannot hold back the disruption in life, but you can control how you respond to it. Releasing your grip that is based on the illusion of control will inevitably help you to release unnecessary stress and anxiety of both past dissapointments and future anxiety. This will help you control how you respond to disruptions in life. The chaos you fear that is falling apart is actually making you wiser, stronger, and more resilient. The turning points that happened in your life caused scars on your heart that may not fully heal but the scar tissue makes you stronger and more equipped to handle the events that you will encounter in the future. The challenges and failures were lessons that taught you and necessary to make you who you are today. In the mist of life's problems, pause, breathe, and ask yourself what this discomfort is teaching you.

You must give the other person space while you decipher if the relationship is worth nurturing. In a job interview, the interviewer gets you to relax so that you talk about yourself without thinking. This method lowers your guard and may reveal insight to the interviewer that will help them decide whether to hire you. The same thing happens with you when you give the other person breathing room to vent, helping you gain insight so that you can decide if the relationship is worth salvaging or not.

Because the poker face expert is the most precious gift if you use it, you learn all you need to know about the person that you are with. Just like bluffing, strategic silence reveals the true essence of the relationship to help you decide on your next move.

Let the person speak because you formulate clues on the best way to respond while you find what they feel on the inside. Johann Wolfgang von Goethe says before you can do something you must first be something. You have to work harder on yourself then you do well on your job, your career, your course, your training, or your volunteer work. Develop yourself first and foremost.

When enlightened, you will get better at letting people express themselves without interrupting them, you will not cut them off, and if you do this then you will remember what you wanted to say right after they make their point.

Your mind is like a vast central knowledge base. You have done so much work on your ability to communicate with people thus far, you learned so much, and you tried so hard, now, all you have to do is let this knowledge and experience complement your thinking with mindsense.

Conclusion

Your moments in the universe begin with developing a life script that you rehearse over and over again until your future becomes your reality. Your life script begins with being the happiest that you can and as grateful as you can be in the moment.

You take yourself there in your mind, walk like you are there, and talk like you are there. In your mind, you are already there.

Earl Nightingale said that this great dream of doing something great, planning a goal, and visualizing your success coupled with process goals or action plans will secure a bright future.

William James argued that your beliefs are those thoughts upon which you are prepared to act. So, you have to act like the person that you want to become. Abe Lincoln taught himself law and was a self-made lawyer. He visioned it, he learned the skills, he acted like a lawyer, and he became a lawyer. People respected his strategic silence while he developed his craft.

Feel the vision in your mind of what you want to become and get emotionally involved in the idea. After a while it will become quite comfortable to secure a great future.

Being too comfortable is also not a good place to be. You have to be doing something that causes a small portion of discomfort. A calling to step into a fuller version of yourself. To trust the unknown and feel that you will be comfortable with your new transformation. This is the gateway to your success in life. You are creating the space for the life that you are searching to create.

***

CHAPTER 7

Moments on Your Ship

Weak people **revenge**. *Strong people* **forgive**. *Intelligent people* **ignore**
—Albert Einstein

Two pillars of resonance: one being meditation and the other being affirmations.

On a ship cruise, you have a choice of a veranda, a portal, or a window. A portal would be a peak at the outside of the ship. A veranda would be a full view of the outer deck and ocean, and a small round porthole window is a section of the ocean captured in a small radius.

Consider the veranda, going deep into the mind and body using meditation. Meditation is the passage to manifestation. Meditation, learning about oneself, reflecting on your best self, and growing your strengths are the keys to mindsense. Meditation could consist of 5 or 10 minutes a day. Just a few moments of silence with no thinking and no thoughts. If a thought occurs, acknowledge it, and then move on from that thought, right back to your meditation. Stay warm as possible because a draft will ruin your focus. Find meaning in the aftermath of the meditation. Meditation through the veranda is a transcendental meditation in which your body is fully relaxed and rejuvenated. You and the universe are one while meditating. You have reached deep relaxation and quieting the mind on the veranda.

Enlightened comes from the inner sense of the energy in your body. The universe is filled with energy. Tapping this universal energy will help you succeed. It is a conduit between the outer universe and the source of the energy within you. When enlightened, you feel more connected to universal power.

Proper sleeping is important to your livelihood. So many people have problems staying asleep or falling into a sound rest. Instead of watching the news before you go to sleep. Listen to music and try to feel grateful before sleeping. This sends out positive vibrations. Send loving vibrations into the world. Try not to hold any grudges with people.

News or intense scenes may impact your sleep. Sleep is the most powerful method of creativity and innovation. Sleeping can be a time of recovery, relaxation, and rejuvenation. Put yourself in a frequency of love and you will attract love into your life. This is inductive reasoning that will feed your thoughts before sleep.

Wallace Wattles said that gratitude is the entire process of mental adjustment. Send love to everyone that you are connected with, even if they are not with you. Do not let the past predict your future. Through repetition of good thoughts and positive accolades to yourself, you can alter what is going on inside your brain.

Play a recording in your mind about how good you are and that you are enough. Alan Watts tells us to say to yourself that "I am enough." I told that to one woman and she said I am more than enough. I recently met a woman that had a tattoo high on her chest and I asked whose name do you have on your chest; she said no name that says, "I am enough." Do you believe in manifestation? Or do you feel this idea of manifesting things into your life is nonsense?

Either way, you begin to believe how good you really are, and the change involves upward growth, expansion of priorities, and this comes across as a full expression of the current moment. You are being in charge of your ship and who gets on it and where it docks.

Through repetition of believing in yourself and feeling that you have already got what you want which will come in the future through manifestation, you visualize through your subconscious and then you manifest it because the universe is on par with what you want and feeds it to you.

Be the solution to your problems. Seek gratitude. Respect yourself enough to walk away from anything that no longer serves you. By forcing yourself to move on, the thoughts about a situation or a person no long takes up space in your mind.

Find manifestation in things that you would like to attract into your life. Darkness leads to rest and recuperation while light gives you energy. The universe offers a source of energy that you join in your deepest sleep pattern. You merge with the universal source of energy. You draw from it the vital energy that sustains you for a short span of time. The dreamless sleep pattern disconnects you from the trials and tribulations that you face on a day-to-day basis. When meditating, the body functions are still operating as normal, and you notice your breathing becomes shallower and you drift into a deep state of relaxation. In the rapid eye movement sleep stage, this state and other comatic states of sleeping, are where the most creativity of the mind exists. You can manifest things in this sleep state and there are no limits to what you can imagine or fixate upon. Your Apple Watch tracks your sleep patterns while wearing it when sleeping.

Great inventors would sleep with a spoon in hand so that they would wake up in the middle of a dream state and record what they were dreaming about when they dropped the spoon.

Thomas Edison and Salvador Dalí reportedly used a sleep technique where they would nap while holding an object like a spoon in their hands. When they began to doze off to sleep, their muscles would relax and the object would fall to the floor, waking them up. Edison famously slept only 3 to 4 hours a night. He regarded sleep as a waste of time.

Sometimes we remember a part of the dream, but it is hard to put all the pieces of the dream back together. Use this inner body mechanism of creative sleep to be a window to manifestation.

There is a breakthrough in what is called "The Genius Wave," in which leading researchers found a new discovery that revs up your brain power. The idea is supported by Stanford University, so it has some merit. It is a 7-minute digital audio track that uses brainwave entertainment technology to activate the Theta Brain Wave by incorporating binaural beats and isochronic tones and operates beneath conscious awareness enabling people to access innate genius abilities associated with the theta state.

FLOW is a state in which we manifest things into our life. There are four science backed ways to turn on your brain power.

- Meditation—twice a day for 20 minutes a day to begin to turn on your Theta Wave.
- Wake up at 4 a.m.—many of us do this due to poor sleep habits but this is an intentional way that many billionaires use to gather great ideas.

- Use a biofeedback machine—In-person sessions could be up to $300 and an in-home biofeedback machine could cost about $7,000.
- Soundwave—Nikola Tesla advises that the secret of the universe is based upon frequency and vibration.

Building on the metaphor of *The Veranda Side of the Ship*, think of your view from your balcony. The vast ocean view of virtually nothing but a large mass of water while you are sitting on a $9 million vessel. With a partner, it could be a very bonding experience, but alone you may feel the burdens of life in your heart and mind through loneliness.

One time, on the *Disney Dream*, an amazing ship with an adult downtown district that offers several bars and music. Truly entertaining.

I was at the bar, and they had a couple event in which they actually did the tarantella, a train like dance to music around the bar. There I was all alone after the I recently lost my marriage, a complicated story about my wife and marriage, but nonetheless, debilitating to my thought process as I see all these couples circling me like an Italian wedding. A wedding I once had with 150 people at the New Jersey shore at a resort hotel called the Breakers in Spring Lake.

Disney cruise ships have Facebook pages set up as private groups for each cruise and I joined. I was trying to connect with the people on the Facebook cruise site. Most people were married with children, good solid families. The ones I would call intact. It was my two daughters and I on the ship. Once the ship left the port, the Facebook group had a few meetups, but the people were not as friendly as I expected them to be. It was important for me to attempt to find friends for my daughters who had just lost their mom, to a great extent; again this is complicated to explain. They made no friends, and I did not connect with anyone on the Facebook group once the ship began sailing.

At one point, a few days into the trip, a young lady walked by me and just looked at me and kept walking. She was alone and not interested in me. She was on her way to the night club, and I was at a bar that she had to walk through to get there. There really was not many people up at this time in the evening. Disney cruises are primary family cruises and people go to bed early. I assumed she was going to the night club that was filled with couples that began to leave after having an awesome time. I was feeling pretty down at this time. I could not stop my thoughts from sending signals to my heart of a not-happening feeling. Being married with children for 14 years had come to a sudden halt. I went back to my room; I opened the door to the veranda, and I looked at the vast ocean in front of me. The entire sky and ocean was pitch black as the ship moved at about 15 knots. It was so dark with only the light from the ship showing the water and light from the ship's bottom and side wake. Nothing to see and just me on a veranda ten stories high, all alone.

For a brief moment I thought of what it would be like to jump overboard. I then knew what it was like to want to kill myself. It was a thought. A feeling. A sensation, a reality that although I would never do it, I thought about it.

I realized that my mind was showing me an image of jumping while my heart was not far apart from that feeling. I said to myself: "Who is this self of mine that is telling me to jump? Is it me or my mind and heart separate from me?" I realized at that moment that I am not my heart and my mind. I am my soul, and my soul is not going to let this mind and heart control my thoughts.

A restlessness set in, there was a shifting of energy, and the universe inside of me began to unravel. My sense of direction in my life felt uncertain because I craved stability, I wanted to know what was next in my life, and I thought my wife would be part of my future. My past seeped into my thoughts and my future was unknown and at this present moment I was totally alone.

The unsettling was a signal from the universe. A sign that I can confront the place in my life that shook up the status quo. We sometimes feel hijacked from ourselves because life hits us like a ton of bricks, but we surrender to the loss and build a new purpose.

With this feeling in the midst of loss, I felt as if the universe was conspiring against me.

I paused, and I stepped back from the chaos in my mind. I let go of the need to control. The chaos in my mind created a space for clarity. I realized that it was purposeful for this breakthrough for me to trust that there was something greater. Life in its infinite wisdom knows when the disruption causes a shift in your thinking. Looking back at that moment of suicidal thoughts was a new beginning for my daughters and me. It was the birthplace of transformation for me.

Just thinking about jumping made me feel how people feel when they lose someone and are at a loss. At the time when I looked at the vast ocean from my veranda, I had this vapid feeling in my gut that made me think, "Why would someone jump off the side of the ship?"

The ship was big and lonely or vast and exhilarating. After that experience, and being very much alone, I continued to try my best to make friends and socialize but to no avail. Mindsense kept me going and I began to be intensely present with myself and my daughters. Cherishing every moment with them. I changed. Although I knew deep down that I would never jump and that just thinking those thoughts was nonsense, it was replacing the nonsense with mindsense that saved me.

I remember telling my sister Patti about it later and she was a bit worried about me. I told her not to worry because I knew at that moment that I had to live in the moment and learned to forget about my past, especially the loss of my wife, but also that trivial moment that included a woman on the ship that I never even met, and the future that has many options but none to focus on at that present moment. It was a purposeful revelation for me, and it prepared me for the new horizon in my life. The universe was not breaking me but rather shaping me.

I survived that brief trauma, and I just recently went on another *Disney Wish* cruise and I had a great time without any thoughts of suicide in my heart, my mind, and my soul.

The veranda was my thinking portal of transformations because I would never want to give up my life and leave my children behind. I also felt that the person that was thinking of jumping was not me; rather, it was the part of me that wanted to be saved from the chaos of my life. The universe had a way of saying something new is coming and I needed to get ready. All I had to do is keep going to face the breakthrough. When the breakthrough was right in front of me, I was so close to transformation that I thought was ever possible.

Although no one wants to truly kill themselves, some do.

For me, it was a cry for help; it was a cry for change. The funny thing is who helped me, no one but the universe. If the change comes quickly enough, then there is no suicide.

Sometimes, your life is hanging on between you and the universe alone. If it is you alone and the only the universe, then you have to have mindsense to survive. The universe does not care about us, so what was it that saved me? I realized that the voice inside of me was not me. I asked myself, "Why would I want to kill myself?"

For a few of my great friends, it was not that easy.

A best friend of mine in my childhood shot his head off at around 30 years of age. Two friends from grammar school shot their heads off, too. One came to me 3 weeks before and mentioned something to me that this may happen to him, and I tried to say as many positive things as possible that I could to let him know that he was loved unconditionally. I wish I could have helped him more because a few weeks later, he died. I was so sad. Another guy from high school took his life. One guy I knew took his life in prison.

These were all great men. Great men! They took their life for whatever reason, no reason in particular; the brain and heart sent troubling thoughts to their heart and soul. The reason should not have been part of their heart, soul, or mind. It was nonsense coming to them from a part of them that was out of control. Rest in peace, my childhood friends, and I will always be sending them and their loved one's positive thoughts.

Who is this voice inside of us that tests us and tells us what we must do? Instead of always seeking something, which is nonsense, we need to start seeing something that makes mindsense. It is called our own *Free Will* and we decide how to use it and what to do with it.

Manifestation can have a negative side to it and the universe does not give a whole lot of care about it either.

You can manifest great things, or you can wallow in negative nonsense. Mindsense is your way to enlightenment and happiness.

Don't let your mind discouraging your thought process. You must detach yourself from the nonsense coming from the part of your brain that stores up all the negativity and losses. Let go of the mental and emotional stress.

Resist the temptation of nonsense and open the veranda portal into the unmanifested because your inner thoughts and resistance cut you off from other people that may not know you but will love you so much when they get to know you and find that you are worthy of their love and affection.

The unmanifested world around you may care a great deal. Manifest hope, love, and compassion. Your survival of mindsense depends on you to go deep within your being to find your inner core. Your VABES (Values, Assumptions, Beliefs, and Expectations about how you see the world and how the world should be).

Tap into your VABES for your own survival. If you are trapped in the wrong VABES, your identity will be vapid, and you may not master true happiness. If you do not love yourself, there can be no love in your heart for others. Your task is not to search for people to love you; your task is to first love yourself unconditionally, then find the love of your life through the veranda portal so that they can enter your cabin and love you there.

Benjamin Franklin, one of the founding fathers of the United States, focused on the moral trait of listening. Listen intently to everything around you. Paying attention to outer silence around you creates an inner silence that awakens your senses and builds your perception. Be aware of your surroundings and be fully alert. Enjoy the simple sounds in the mist or directly around you.

When my mom was buried, my cousin Nick Fotiu, the NFL hockey player, her godson, brought two doves to the funeral. He released them into the wild. One flew away and the other sat on a tree branch above the crowd at the cemetery. When the priest stated that my mom's soul had gone to heaven, a few trees moved above us, which my cousin Tracy also noticed.

Notice everything and do not waste a moment of your life. Every sound. Every word.

Every sound comes from some silence somewhere, once drawn, fades back into the silence. Silence is your friend; stillness is your way of being. Once you master this technique of meditating and contemplating in the moment, you will become more enlightened, more aware. You will feel more intelligent, and you will manifest things.

Being aware of your space and using every bit of it to your advantage because you exist as a ball of energy in the universe. Find every nook and cranny in your home and use it. Have a special chair, a quiet space, a view of nature, find it and make that your creative space.

At work, build a space with the things you love, at home build unique reminders of what you do and the places that you have traveled. My sister

Patti's home is like a museum of her travels and livelihood of her family over the years. Every room, every wall, every counter has a cherished memory. The door of her refrigerator is filled with icons of all her travels, both domestic and abroad.

Create your space, not only the physical space in which you dwell but also the space in your mind. Use your space to your advantage and you can manifest anything. Manifest your next love partner, manifest your next job opportunity, manifest your next fun and exciting adventure.

Conclusion

Wayne Dyer argues that it is not the snake that bites the person that kills them, it is the venom inside the snake that kills them.

Einstein thought that space and time are intertwined in an infinite fabric like an outstretched blanket.

In order to know where you are on your ship, you have to be aware of who you let on and where you are headed. This space and time continuum is very important to not only your livelihood but also to your travels, to your trials, and to your tribulations. Cherish your space.

Carl Jung provides a perspective on death and dying. A Jungian perspective is that death is inevitable. The one thing we all know and agree upon is that we are going to die someday. Death is inevitable and to think otherwise is to live in denial. Death is psychologically as important as birth and, like it, is an integral part of life. Putting death off by taking care of yourself, meditating, relaxing, and enjoying life is what matters most.

Be enlightened and awake each moment. Do not worry about anything. You control the steering wheel of your ship, its course, and the passengers that you let on. Spend every single moment the best that you can.

***

CHAPTER 8

Moments of Enlightenment

I have a limited amount of time left on this planet and I am not going to spend it being a watered-down version of myself just so that people can like me

—Bree Christina

You cannot stop the future, you cannot rewind the past, the only way to learn the secret, is to press play

—Jay Asher

Opening Vignette—The Cookie Thief by Valerie Cox—found on the public domain

A woman was waiting at an airport one night,
With several long hours before her flight.
She hunted for a book in the airport shop,
Bought a bag of cookies and found a place to drop.
She was engrossed in her book but happened to see,
That the man beside her as bold as could be,
Grabbed a cookie or two from the bag between,
Which she tried to ignore to avoid a scene.
She read, munched cookies, and watched the clock,
As this gutsy "cookie thief" diminished her stock.
She was getting more irritated as the minutes ticked by,
Thinking "If I wasn't so nice I'd blacken his eye!"
With each cookie she took, he took one too.
And when only one was left, she wondered what he'd do.
With a smile on his face and a nervous laugh,
He took the last cookie and broke it in half.

He offered her half, as he ate the other.
She snatched it from him and thought, "Oh brother,
This guy has some nerve, and he's also rude,
Why, he didn't even show any gratitude!"
She had never known when she had been so galled,
And sighed with relief when her flight was called.
She gathered her belongings and headed for the gate,
Refusing to look back at the "thieving ingrate."
She boarded the plane and sank in her seat,
Then sought her book, which was almost complete.
As she reached in her baggage, she gasped with surprise.
There was her bag of cookies in front of her eyes!
"If mine are here," she moaned with despair
"Then the others were his and he tried to share!"
Too late to apologize, she realized with grief,
That she was the rude one, the ingrate, the thief.

***

Thinking inside-out instead of outside-in is the only way to live your life. Changing your perception to an inside-out viewpoint can help you with mindsense.

- Shift your perception to gratitude and the positive things in your life.
- Communicate with the unseen world that we call the universe.
- Innovate and be creative to enable you to create the world you want.
- Change the perception of yourself and the world changes with you.
- Master time. Unfortunately, time cannot be managed, you must manage the activities in the time allotted to you each moment.
- Master the art of meditation.
- Be more productive and effective. Efficiency is sometimes overvalued to effectiveness. You can be efficient and get up and feel that you are productive but are you effective? The harder and more effective you work on yourself, the luckier you get, and the more opportunities come your way.

- Think logically.
- Change your focus on money. Don't focus on lack, focus on abundance.

We all have some type of trauma that we have dealt with which is stored in the compartmentalization of our mind. Many people feel that they will never forget, they will always be sad. This is not true.

You are your own person, and you do not need validation from another person.

A 9-year-old boy was criticized for doodling in class; his mom and dad encouraged him to continue his creativity. One of the young boy's teachers recognized his talent and posted his work on Instagram. His drawings caught the eye of the 'Number 4' restaurant, which asked him to come over and decorate their walls with his doodles. Now, his dad drives him there so he can draw as much as he likes. Who knew that drawing in an after-class program would lead Joe to get his first job at barely 9 years old? Joe is on his way to be an artist that is well recognized at such a young age for going against the grain.

The mind and your thoughts are your mindset, sometimes you can control your thoughts and sometimes you just have to let the thoughts run their course. Ask yourself, "What is this thought teaching me? Why now, how can I see why the thought is appearing to my mind right now?" Only mindsense can help you live in the moment.

The moment may be filled with nothing but sitting on the couch, but it is still your moment, be alive in it. Cherish it!

Vignette—Love of Your Life

Cyndy, a Fort Myers Florida resident, told me that I can tell her story.

She was married for many years after living with the same man for 18 years. When they got married, she said, "I do," and he said, "I don't." They lasted married for about 10 years or so and broke up.

Being single or separated, she went onto a dating site for seniors and met a man named Andy. Andy had just lost his mom, and he was quiet, did not smile, and was very sad. Cyndy lit him up.

Andy was so happy after meeting Cyndy, that he spoke of her name to his sons 10 or 12 times a day. Andy and Cyndy traveled to many countries together and they were so happy for a year or so.

Andy was in great shape. He ran 6 miles a day, walked at night and he just went to the doctor and had a clean bill of health. Andy wanted to go on a cruise. In order to go on a cruise, Andy and Cyndy had to get the COVID-19 shot. They did.

A month later, while hugging Cyndy watching television, Andy died in Cyndy's arms with a sudden cardiac arrest. No one truly knows why he suddenly died. Just as he died, Cyndy was crying by his side. The police officer stood over the body on the living room floor and Cyndy could not go near him until the funeral director examined the body.

The police officer asked Cyndy if Andy recently got the COVID-19 shot, she said yes. The police officer mentioned that we used to see many people in the obituary dying of old age but now we see the ages getting younger.

Send good thoughts to Cyndy wishing that she can find the love of her life once again.

The epilogue of this story is that it took a whole year for her to get over that relationship and look for love. Thoughts linger and time heals.

***

Finding love in your life for some people could be a bit challenging. Some people call themselves hopeless romantics.

Just like your goals and aspirations, the universe does not give a damn about your love life. You have to expect love and be loved to attract it to you. If you are a narcissist, selfish, or arrogant it may be complicated to find love.

Loving yourself first and then loving others unconditionally could help. The point is to be patient and not be needy. No one wants a man or woman that is needy. Have people join your life and do not let them rule it and never try to rule other people's life either.

If compatibility is not combined with chemistry and adaptability, love may be elusive.

There are the things you can say that you love about someone else and then ask them what type of love you want. Here is a guide map focusing on the following attributes to build, keep, and nurture your love.

What I Like About You:
- Your morals and your concern for others
- Your infectious sense of humor
- Your warmth
- Your insightful business sense
- Your planning and personal discipline skills
- Your ability to motivate others (including me) toward their or my best professional and personal goals
- Your concern for your family and their well-being
- Your respect for the elderly
- Your belief in me and all that I am capable of accomplishing in this world

What I Would Like from You:
- Daily showing of physical affection, (nods, kisses, hugs, general touches for no particular reason)
- Giving help or offering to help when not asked
- Periodic check on my well-being (physical and emotional)
- Listening to my concerns without judgment
- Showing appreciation for the little things I do
- Allowing me to have my own judgments without needing you to influence my thoughts and actions
- Compromise so that neither one of us has to be right or wrong
- Love must be given unconditionally and without any recourse for reciprocation

Addiction can also happen in love. First and foremost, we must never appear needy of another person. We want them in our lives, but we should not be needy of them. It is not that you do not want them in your life but needing someone to make you whole will only disappoint you.

Always be nice to everyone, never ghost a person, just let them know that you must move on for whatever reason. Narcissists do not care about one particular person and feel that everyone is replaceable.

Finding love is not easy, we all know that. As Shakespeare says, it is better to love and lose that love than to never love at all.

To avoid the addictive state of love, you must be present in the moment. Attract people into your life and set boundaries. Give love without trying to get anything in return. This can make a profound difference in a relationship.

With mindsense, you learn to focus on the current moment and do not let distractions take away from that moment. Sure, you plan your next move, your next date, your next goal to feel better and look healthier, but all this is done in the current moment.

Be careful as you venture into another bad relationship because your picker may be off. You maybe selecting the wrong people into your life for whatever reason. Fight the thoughts of brining the wrong person into your life.

Let go of distractions and find a way to just live in the present moment. The next moments that you choose to share with someone will be special moments for both them and you.

Conclusion

To go from doing what you have always done in your life to enlightenment is possible. Set your mind and your thoughts to support the current moment. You must make the moment your entire life.

Enlightened relationships will come when you are used to being in the present moment. Be happy being alone.

Women tend to be stronger than men and they are closer to enlightenment. Some men have this illusion that a woman cooks, cleans, and takes care of the household while they play in their man cave. Women have always been oppressed and held back by both men and society throughout centuries. Through this strife, women have become more enlightened.

While woman are more enlightened than men, they often do not find a purpose in life as easy as men do. Finding your purpose in life must not be gender specific. Everyone needs to find some purpose in their life.

The ego can stop people from feeling enlightened because it wants safety and status quo. Shut down that negative dialogue with your mind and thoughts.

The ego in some countries, for example, the UK, has taken a back seat to marriage in lieu of dating. Statistics are showing that people want to remain single, not so much alone, but single and unmarried. In 2022, over 28.9 million people in England and Wales were single, compared to 24 million who were married. The point of the matter is that marriage may not be for everyone.

The universe does not give a heck about you but it is all you have to work with so use it to your advantage by sending out love and be love and watch it attract love to you. Remember the code of finding love:

- The universe helps those who help themselves.
- Nothing ventured, nothing gained.
- Where there is a will there is a way.
- Good things come to those who wait.
- When one door closes another door opens.
- If you love someone, let them go, if they come back its beautiful.
- It is better to love and lose than to never love at all.
- You are never a hopeless romantic, you are a loving person.

Captain Abrashoff clarified in his book *It's Your Ship*.

In June 1997, Captain D. Michael Abrashoff boarded the USS Benfold; he was the new commanding officer. The USS Benfold, a guided missile destroyer, was staffed with 310 sailors. This was Abrashoff's first sea command, so he was undoubtedly anxious as he walked onto the ship. Captain Abrashoff commanded his ship adhering to the following premises:

1. Your life, the partner you select, and your career are your ship.
2. You are the Captain of your ship, your career, and your relationship.
3. You decide the purpose of your ship, your life, and the partner that you select.
4. You decide the rules on board your ship, your extent to care about your partner, and your career.
5. You decide whom to invite on board your ship, the people that will enhance your relationship and not take away from your partner, your career, and your life.
6. You decide how fast you want to go in your relationship, how far you want to take it, how long you want to stay in your career, and when you will retire.

7. You decide what ports to pull into, what vacations to take, what trips to plan, what quality time to utilize, and how long you want to stay in those ports.

8. You decide the condition of your ship when you step off. You decide the condition of your dwelling, your garden, your home. It's really up to you and all these decisions will help you with your enlightenment and your mindsense.

The key is to be consistent in love and ascertain enlightenment first in yourself and then in others. Be consistent when in a relationship and show intention.

***

CHAPTER 9

Moments of Going with the Flow

Life is not a matter of milestones, but of the moments in each milestone
—Rose Kennedy

Going with the flow is making your positive thoughts in the moment a habit for life. Ignoring your thoughts is not going to be helpful when seeking enlightenment and mindsense.

Ignorance of enlightenment inevitably leads to worry, doubt, fear, anxiety, depression, and ultimately, on a larger spectrum, disease and disintegration. The negative energy within and thru the body which begins to set the vibration known as anxiety causes psychological suffering. Many of us have some form of anxiety.

Anxiety is generally suppressed in most of us, and this suppression may turn into depression if not monitored. The key is to keep your worry to a minimum and focus on what you have full control over which is your moment-to-moment thoughts.

Wayne Dyer said that he can eliminate all your worries. He argues that if you can control something, then do not worry about because you can control it, and if you cannot control something, do not worry about it because you cannot control it. This idea by Wayne, may eliminate some of your worries but in reality, the things that you cannot control still may worry you. With mindsense, you use your knowledge and experience to help you focus on your worrying.

Knowledge is a universal gift given to humans more than any other species in the world. Knowledge is the positive path to enlightenment.

You must study and know what to study by guiding yourself based on your strengths. The Reflected Best Self Exercise establishes your true strengths and how you can capitalize and develop them.

Organize knowledge intelligently so that you can direct yourself on how you will go about learning and growing. The opposite of doubt and worry is understanding, and this leads to positivity. Understanding yourself by following your own conscious effort gives into the call of the universal power. This heightened self-awareness give you faith and hope. Faith is the ability to see the invisible. You see yourself being what you want to become and then your become it.

For a wine connoisseur, wine ripens, they drink it; some wine needs to be the ripest, they wait for it; some they may never get to drink because the date may be beyond their life span. Think carefully about your next track to learning and growing and grow with confidence, living each moment with joy and happiness. Work hard and play hard. Work smarter, not harder.

We sometimes have to deal with crisis intervention more than we expect today. During Hurricane Ian, in Fort Myers, Florida in 2023, people were faced with devastation. One man was on a rooftop 12 ft high for 4 days and he watched people float by and other people on boats trying to get to a higher elevation.

While this act of nature is alarming to anyone, as bad as it is, we learn from it. Victor Frankl, as mentioned in earlier chapters, was devastated by the German concentration camps, but he never gave in, and he was able to help millions of people after surviving himself.

Mihaly Csikszentmihalyi became curious about happiness after seeing the pain and suffering of Europeans around him during World War II. He found that many were unable to live contentedly after losing their jobs, homes, and general security during the war. These observations led him to become curious about what made life worth living, and he began to explore art, philosophy, and religion as he sought answers. His answers have helped so many people as he calls his idea "*FLOW.*" Csikszentmihalyi's studies on flow included interviews with scientists, athletes, musicians, artists, business executives and others—particularly creative professionals—because he wanted to know when they experienced optimal performance levels and how they felt. His research led him to conclude that happiness is an internal state of being, and it is a matter of external factors.

Master the art of flow to live in consciousness and be more enlightened in the moment. When in a FLOW state:

> *Time warps distorting space and time (sometimes you slow things down to ensure that you are capturing every moment and sometimes you increase the pace to cover as much as you can as fast as you can, so you capitalize on the time) Managing time helps us live better in the moments with others, with ourselves, and with nature.*

The flow state helps us lose sense of our selves because sometimes the self is debilitated with worry and concern for things that may not matter as much as they truly do. This type of worry is consuming and will take away from the moment.

Intense focus in intervals can restore the creative mind of the childlike imagination within you. Children, to some extent, have no inhibitions and simply enjoy life. Even failure is not an option for children. Up to the age of 3 a child fails often when they try to walk. Then they experience what Price Pritchett calls a quantum leap. They learn to walk. You can create a quantum leap goal for yourself now. However, you must keep your ego at bay because it may try to hold you back from taking the risk of a quantum leap goal.

Always attempt to perform at your highest level. When you do something do it with all your might. No slacking. No limits. Just do it. If the results do not compare to others doing the same thing, ignore that, just keep up the persistence to reach your internal and external highest level. Even in the old west, there was always someone faster and better gunfighter than the new or up-and-coming outlaw. The same with card playing, which offers a variety of great players that may be excellent at strategy and bluffing. There may always be someone with more knowledge and experience than you but that should not hold you back.

Having a sense of awareness is key to your success. Know thyself, as mentioned in earlier chapters is so profound. Know what you are good at, your strengths, and build upon them. Never let your effort go unrecognized within your personal contributions to your innovativeness and creativity. Even when you are not recognized by others, recognize yourself.

Find mentors, even if you cannot reach them personally, watch their videos and be like a sponge that soaks up knowledge.

Regain a larger sense of self. Walk around with a chip on your shoulder, you are alive, you are healthy, and most important, you are more than enough.

Stand straight, carry yourself well. Never compare yourself to others that learned something before you or have learned a great deal before you, just compare yourself to your increased potential and incremental improvement. Learn from people with knowledge whenever you can but do not compare yourself to them in a negative way.

Bruce Lee once showed up at a great master's home for tea. They spoke before the tea came to the table by a geisha girl. The master asked the girl not to pour. Bruce was still talking about his great new style Jeet Kun Do. The master poured the tea, first in his own cup up to the top, and then he poured more, and kept pouring the tea into Bruce's cup until the cup overflowed with the tea.

"Master, the tea is overflowing," said Bruce respectfully.

"Your cup is too full, you must empty your cup so that you can learn," explained the master with a stern look in his eye.

Bruce realized that perhaps he was too excited and was too eager to learn from the great master. The master went on to teach Bruce to live strongly in the moment and enjoy his life to the fullest each moment and not be so full of himself.

Bruce failed in that first meeting with that master. Sometimes failure teaches us to fail forward. John Maxwell, the great leadership trainer, said, "Fail early, fail often, but always fail forward." Maxwell argued that failing forward is all about iteration, about risking failure (with a small and controlled scope of impact) in order to eventually achieve success. Failing first, you learn how to be better earlier, fail often to learn and grow, fail forward so that you can begin at a new and better place.

Sim Sitkin, a Duke's Fuqua School of Business professor of leadership, said, at an Academy of Management meeting, that he tells his students that they cannot be leaders because they never failed at anything. He let them talk among themselves about that premonition of failing and the students began to argue about who failed the most and how often.

Your ego is the drama center of your body. It will deflect failure as something to avoid at all costs. Some people do not care about the ego and will fall into the clutches of their own ego, while others will laugh at the ego as an echo so low that they cannot hear it.

Can you think of anyone in the world more important than you are right now? If you answered no, your ego is functioning pretty well. We may think that other people that we love or care for are more important than us, but our ego will keep us intact and let us know differently. In this case, the ego is correct because taking care of yourself first will trickle down to the ones you love and care for.

Your ego may cause you to cut your nose to spite your face. Hate certainly comes from your ego. Ego can sometimes bring on emotional damage and at its worst, and in some cases, the ego can cause people to act out in physical violence. I remember once watching a guy want to fight in a nightclub. I tried to calm him down and he told me, "He can't beat me." I looked at him sadly as his ego would probably land him in jail.

We go through cycles of life that impact the moments in our life. Carl Jung, the renowned psychologist founded the *Stages of Life* which are composed of five levels. He uses a metaphor of Sunrise to Sunset. The first half of life is from birth to middle age and the second half of life spans from around 40 years of age until death. The bulk of work to be done in the first half of life entails the development of you as a person, while in the second half of life, you begin to focus inwardly to achieve individuation. To achieve this, it is necessary to revisit the big dreams that inspired you during your childhood.

The key thing is to take every stage in life for what it gave you and what you did and could continue to do now. At each stage of your life, stay in the moment, stay enlightened, and have mindsense.

Conclusion

Going with the flow is a conscious thought pattern that helps you live in the moment. Never doubt the moment you are in and the capacity that you have to continue your journey of learning, growing, simply existing, or sharing time with others.

In the moment, continuously conduct a *Want-Gap Analysis* to relinquish negativity, and ensure positive psychology.

Negative wants and desires may continue to resonate from your ego pushing and pulling you in many directions. Some good some bad. You must attempt to find a way to block your ego, or it could destroy your moment. Negativeness comes from not only what you have been through but from years of despair in your ancestral heritage. You may carry the burden of generations before you, and if you do this you will inevitably be troubled with negativity.

To offset this genetic hardware that you inherited, hang with your pets, visit nature often, sit in silence, and meditate.

Be in the room with loved ones even if you are not sharing conversation. With mindsense, the future is not the result of choices among alternative paths offered in the present moment. The present moment is just that and you must cherish that moment. You may find yourself diligently working or avoiding a lecture by a professor, leader, parent, or partner, always try to remember to focus back on the current moment and give your full attention to the person that you are sharing the moment with.

When time allows, use the present moment as a place where you create what you desire in your future and plan how to get there. Plan what you need to manifest to get there in the current moment.

The current moment is created first in your mind and developed from your free will. Then you create the next execution which will be in a future moment. This moment can be planned but it will not happen until the actual moment in the future. Create your future using mindsense and enlightenment.

Remember the Zen master that takes the middle ground. If you desire something so much, try not to desire it. However, this may cause you to desire it more. Try not to desire it more. The basic premise here is that you realize that you will have desires, and that you will have to let them be. Take the middle ground in your moments like Zen masters do.

People only see the tip of you as an iceberg. You will be judged by people that feel they are smarter than you or do not see your potential. That is OK. You know your potential and that is all that matters.

You have the ability to manifest things, you are truly enlightened, and your mindsense takes you far beyond the tip of the iceberg. Your inner core is fully developed, and you are enlightened.

Exist in the moment at Level Three Personal Leadership.

At Level One personal leadership, people see what you say and do, and they see enough for them to judge you.

At Level Two personal leadership, you are acting from a thought and thinking process, but at Level Three you tap into your true beliefs that are semiconscious to unconscious. These beliefs of yours are the core center of your true enlightenment. At this point in your enlightenment, you are at the core of the universe.

Do not let people effect your version at the surface level because must deeper are your true perspectives on life in which they may be able to see. You have VABES on every topic and subject and that makes you a unique and authentic individual.

The way to your personal leadership is your own philosophy of enlightenment and that is your own Level Three Personal Leadership.

At Level Three Personal Leadership, you are fully aware of your mind, your heart, and your soul.

You are much more than the surface level as shown as the tip of you as an iceberg. When you consider yourself a full iceberg, you have deep core beliefs that make you special and enlightened that begin at the bottom of the iceberg to the tip. Although people may not see this greatness in you, the fact of the matter is that you see your potential and how great you truly are, and that is all that matters.

***

CHAPTER 10

Give in to the Moment

Dwell on the reward and you move toward it, dwell on the penalty and you move toward it

—*Dennis Waitley*

Having trust and faith in the moment is very important to becoming more enlightened. With faith and trust, you can also believe the incredible things that can happen in your life. The next time a door closes, and you have no response or awareness of what happened, trust in universe that this door needed to be closed so that you can become better and stronger and with more resolve.

Just as the caterpillar resolves to the cocoon to later become a butterfly, you too will always turn out better after a loss or failure. All you have to do is trust the process of change and renewal.

Zig Zigler and Jim Rohn, two prominent personal development gurus, argue that if you can help the masses of people get what they want, then you can get everything you want.

If you see the invisible power of the universe as your segway to manifesting what you want, then you can ascertain it and bring whatever you desire to the forefront of your life. You must believe this for it to happen. Trust in the knowledge of intuition and not noise or dialogue of nonsense. There is nothing to fear, silence is a mirror reflecting back to you who you are. Lean into the loneliness and despair. Ask yourself, "What is this silence trying to show me? What strength is waiting to be discovered within me?" Like seeds waiting for the right time for enough light and water to sprout.

You must see it in your conscious mind with your imagination. With knowledge of the universe being on purpose, the understanding of this brings you faith and trust. You must have faith and trust in the expression of what you see in the mind of your future self through visualizing that you already have it. This expression turns to acceleration which then turns to creation. That is manifesting and that is mindsense. You can manifest anything that you want in your life. You just have to truly want it. You must be patient, however. Manifesting may take time while the process is in play.

The world is made to help you enjoy yourself. This is not taught in school. You have not learned the very simple art of living in the moment. You consider what you need and then get on with living in the moment. It is simple to enjoy watching the most minute things. Sun on your face. A nice breeze. A warm shower. Having gratitude is key. The importance of the littlest things are felt in the moment.

We confuse growing and progressing with living in the moment. You do not need to continuously work for the future. Work for the moment that you are in right now. Plan accordingly, but do this in the current moment.

Once you know you want something, then you begin the habitual task by reinforcing the positive. Try not to reinforce the negative. Negative thoughts will sink into your mind because that is your EGO trying to hold you back. The EGO is most powerful. The EGO helps us at certain times, but it also could hinder your creativity and stop you manifesting.

You have to attempt to fix the habit of only focusing on the future and get off the idea of the rat-race. Don't get stuck in the subconscious mind. Even if you still win the so-called rat-race, even as a winner you will still be a rat.

Change your brain as a habit of not only caring about your money. Once you get into the habit of living in the moment, it is then programmed into your subconscious mind. The habit through repetition will help you change your habits. Money is bookkeeping and taxation and it is just a flow of wealth, and a continuous fixation on money will lead to stress and it will keep you from moving toward progress on your personal development.

Money will come as you focus on the moment and do your job and go about learning and developing. The idea of money coming into your life, and the future focus of having abundance are the same. Instead of focusing on the future, live now in the moment and work hard on personal development.

Don't waste your life; true waste is on the brink of self-awareness. Some day you will live a certain way. Life's magic is here in the laughter of friends and the joy that are commonly taken for granted.

Use cue cards and visualize them in the morning and night and even throughout the day. This still works. Read them out loud to yourself. You have to create a habit of repetition, read it and then read it again, and again. Repetition is key to secure it in your mind.

The habit of visualizing the right things will help change the program of your mind through your subconscious which will then be part of your conscious thought.

What do you really want? You may not be able to do something right at the moment. But if you can see that you can do it in the future, you are holding the image of possibility. Your mind does not know the difference between having it or not, but the mind does know what it feels like to have what you want. You must program this feeling into your mind through repetition.

If you are holding the image of poverty, then you will never reach prosperity.

Hold the image of abundance and doing great and being great. Hold the image in your mind of doing what you love so well that people admire you.

My father told me at a very young age to walk around like you have a chip on your shoulder son because you are a good looking, handsome, and a smart man with a good build. This helped my self-esteem greatly as a young man.

- Develop an awareness of your true potential which may be your internal compass set on your true north. The compass of the heart is a form of communication that exists between the brain and the heart through the nerves, according to James Doty, the author of the book titled *Mind Magic*. Doty argues that the heart sends far more signals to the brain than what the brain sends to the heart. This is important to know because the heart has more of a neural connection than the heart. Based on this logic, go with both your heart and mind but your heart will place your compass in the right direction.

- Act as if you have what you want right now.
- Make a decision to form a habit of ascertaining what you want. Visualization is not enough. Set process and action goals to achieve your goals.
- Make a total commitment to developing your mind to focus on what you want.
- Be accountable by still doing the things that you have to do on a necessary basis throughout your day but then add this habitual thinking to your repertoire. Also, habit stacking works too, as you make your coffee or tea, plan your day.
- Focus on your target, you will have many targets, attempt to give equal time to each target to manifest all of them at the same time. Although they may appear at different times, once you ascertain one, you can focus more on the other targets.
- Be disciplined. Work hard each day like clockwork with a strong desire to succeed in life.
- Be a supervisor of your life. Supervisors have super vision and can see what they need to do and then do it.

It's time to give in to your moment. Say to yourself, "I am Alive!"

Sylvester Stallone says, "It is what it is!" Many people feel that a moment is just that, but it may be your most important moment in life. Think of a time when you met someone or agreed on a project that got you excited. Remember that moment? Great moments will come, and you must be ready when they do.

It is very important that you are able to deal with acceptance of the present moment. Surrender your ill feeling toward others. When you surrender into the moment, you already changed your goal to be happy and content. It is not easy, but it comes naturally after a while. Opposing the flow of the moment stops you from living your best self. Accept the present moment unconditionally and without reservation.

The Marilyn Monroe syndrome is often looked upon as a life in which nonsense set into her thoughts and behavior. Marilyn was one of the most famous actress in the United States and known worldwide. Marilyn was so beautiful and attractive that people lined up to see her. Some people talked about her dress size or her lack of intelligence, but everyone agrees that she reached stardom and was famous. Marilyn lived her life like a candle in the wind according to the lyrics of *Elton John*. Do not go about your life like a candle in the wind. Instead, believe in manifestation.

Jim Carrey, the famous actor, covered the art of manifestation in his career.

> I have an insane belief in my own ability to manifest things. I believe it is incredibly complete sanity. I believe we are creators, and I believe that we create with every thought and every word that every moment is pregnant with the next moment in our life. We all start out with a false belief about ourselves. With some untrue thing that we believe as we walk through our lives saying to ourselves that we are not worthy, that, perhaps we are not lovable, or that we are going to fail at something. Whatever your mistaken belief about yourself is, you form a personality around that. I form the characters I play that way.

Do not let the world determine your dreams. Manifest them using mindsense.

Sometimes you just have to be able to say no with confidence. I call it bowing out gracefully. If people are taking advantage of you, let them know, let them know that you will not tolerate that behavior. Set boundaries and move on. Then go about attracting positive people in your life.

Some of us feel pain in our bodies of some type. According to Joe Dispenza, the new popular self-help guru, people heal themselves through meditation and reprogramming their mind.

According to Luther West, in an article published in 2023, for many who suffer from illness, chronic pain, or emotional trauma, healing can seem out of reach. We might feel stuck in broken patterns, believing our situation to be permanent. Yet possibilities exist to profoundly transform our relationship to afflictions when we leverage the wisdom of the body, mind, and spirit.

Meditation teacher Dr. Joe Dispenza created specific meditations to catalyze deep healing and rewire a person's thinking. West argues that by meeting pain with conscious presence instead of resistance, true alchemy happens. You have to be willing to accept Joe's theory of healing. If so, you may have some luck because it is mind over matter.

Eckhart Tolle argues that the belief that you are sick and your belief that this condition continues to bother you, may empower the feeling of pain. Thinking this way may make a seemingly solid reality out of a temporary imbalance that may dissipate on its own over time.

The one thing that all pop psychologists and enlightened self-help gurus believe is that meditation is a way of life.

When and if disaster strikes, the thoughts coming from the mind are projected into the future. Since you only have the present moment, it is better to be well prepared and in a secure place to lessen your trauma and troubles. Whatever you decide to do, make every moment count by preparing, being vigilant, and protecting the people you love.

I remember one day I lived in Edison, New Jersey, and I was cooking veal piccata, which is a stove top dish with wine, butter, and lemon. I threw something outside the front door, and it closed behind me. I realized that I had my pajamas on and no key. No one else was home. I walked to the back of my home and looked in through the kitchen window. After a few moments of contemplating my options, I noticed a flame from the veal sauce cooking down. I quickly busted the window with my bare hands, it smashed, I climbed in and saved my home. Be vigilant and act quickly in the moment when necessary.

So how do we deal with our difficult illness? I remember my Uncle Reid's mom was dying and I just happened to be there visiting in Virginia, in the United States of America. She was a beautiful soul, and she prayed to all the statues of saints in her room knowing that someday she will pass. Some people know that when the time comes that they will accept it realizing that they will be in a better place.

My uncle Michael, one of my favorite uncles whom I was named after, would wake up for an hour a day during his later years of life. His beautiful wife, my Aunt Mary, and my cousins Michelle and Phyllis would dote over him for that hour out of their love for him. Uncle Michael, at some point, told his loved ones how he felt about them, that he loved them dearly and that he had a great life, knowing his time was coming to pass away. Imagine how important those moments of waking are at that time in your life. We can feel that same feeling now as we are young and vibrant. Each moment counts, don't waste it.

My father's brother Jimmy, one of the middle brothers but well loved by his mom, was told in the hospital that if he took his leg off, he would live. He denied cutting off his leg because he felt his wife was already in a wheelchair and he did not want to burden her in any way. He died.

Sometimes we see our life passing on. In this case, some of us transform our suffering into some sort of peace of mind.

My mom did not want anyone to take care of her in her later years. She wanted a quick death without anyone taking care of her. She died in the bathroom. By the time my dad found her and the ambulance eventually came, she was brain dead.

Surrender each moment to the reality of that moment. We know we will die someday, but we just push off the date for as long as we can. If you find someone you love, love them dearly and unconditionally because moments with them are precious.

Conclusion

This is your life, and you have the power to choose what your life is like. You are compelled to think, feel, and act in certain ways according your VABES (values, assumptions, beliefs, and expectations about how you perceive the world is and how it should be). Your mind has already been programmed and it is your turn to recondition your mind, your thoughts, and your behavior.

Doty, in his book, *Mind Magic*, argues that the universe does not care a bit about you. Thus, work with the universal laws that govern the growth of your enlightenment and consciousness.

Let the universe guide you to your destiny and if someone does not want to join you, keep going, don't look back, and feel good about going into the new. Give into the moment and select who you want to share that moment with.

***

CHAPTER 11

Your Awesome Power to Change the Moment

Past experiences are our baggage for the future. We have learned that the secret of our survival is our work and our effort. Yes, I am a statue of success, but I did not get this title easily. I have put forty years of continuous effort into it. I am sure that if you are not afraid of problems, one day this title will be yours

—Lee Iacocca, Chief Executive Officer

Become the individual that you want to become and have the attitude of already being that person. Attempt to learn everything about your work. Learn both depth and breadth of every aspect of your business. Know everything about the industry you are in or want to join. Try to know everything about the people that report to you by first knowing everything about yourself.

Earl Nightingale made a fortune on his speech called Acres of Diamonds. He told a story of a farmer in Africa that sat on land for many years, the farmer desired to find diamonds which he felt were in the vicinity of his property. He searched and searched for gold until he was poor and had no money. After feeling as if he was a failure, he took his own life by jumping off a cliff and dying.

After his death, his family settled his estate and his property was sold. The new owner lived on the property for a long time. After some inclement weather came through his property, the damage to his property caused a break in the stream that went directly through the farm.

The new owner noticed a rock that was very awkward, quite huge, and protruded above the streaming water. After careful inspection, the rock in the stream turned out to be a diamond. The new owner was now rich.

The man that took his own life in despair was sitting on acres of diamonds. Based on this story, Earl made a fortune telling people that you may be sitting on acres of diamonds, and you are totally unaware of it.

Inside of each of you are acres of diamonds that you have to tap into and polish and use.—Earl Nightingale

You may have enormous potential. People tend to focus on the mundane life that they live until something happens that sets them off course. You are often overthinking things in your mind way too much.

As a fatalist, you attempt to create monologues in your thinking and these narratives set the precedent for your day-to-day moments of negativity in your life which makes your day be less enjoyable. The funny thing about the fatalist perspective is that it cannot survive unless you let it.

Overthinking is prompted directly after an episode takes place in your life that is particularly strong and, therefore, it is at the forefront of your thinking, but this eventually fades as the recency effect dissipates. The situation becomes a short fleeting thought in the mind after a while. This is how mindsense works. The thought must run its course, and it is hard to control at first. Over time, you will wonder why you let that thought bother you so much.

Frankie Prof, my father, once said: "This too shall pass, son, this too shall pass." After something traumatic happened in my life. He continued: "No matter how bad this looks at the time, it is not as bad as it seems to be."

However, this is not always followed in our hearts and minds, and it is not easy to just tell someone something and expect to heal them. Our thoughts get the best of us all the time. There is hope, however, we can simply be present.

Our focus of climbing the latter and awaiting the next grandiose thing that we are fixated on in our life is your problem of always wanting more. We can stop this thought process by savoring the moments and simple pleasures. Listen to your inner desires and your inner purpose in life.

Some people look angry, and you ask them why they look so angry, and they say:

"I am not angry," in a captivating tone.

The key is to realize that the anger that you are feeling is all in your mind. Address the anger. You can say, yes, I feel angry. Knowing that the anger is temporary.

We creatively destroy our way of thinking with ego generated thoughts and actions. Once this passes, we can look back and feel how foolish we were at that time. The anger, however, is real. Just deal with it.

Unfortunately, we tend to hate too much and wish terrible things to happen to people that hurt us. This is not good for your inner dialogue with yourself. If you feel ill will toward someone, realize that you must have unconditional love toward everyone as much as possible.

In many cases, you are your own worst critic. Your inflated ego tells you about your loss, how you lost it, and what you did wrong in order to cause the loss. This worry is played out in your mind repeatedly.

It is as if someone has a camera on you and is filming you. People are not watching the stupid things that you say or the idiotic things that you may have done.

This is your mind filming yourself while no one is watching anything that you did wrong. This is where the despair happens to you, and it is all nonsense. You build your own inner self-awareness, and you do not need anyone to validate your opinion of yourself.

Surround yourself with positive people that care about you.

Wanda Sykes, an actor and comedian, talks about how women think in a comedic role:

Women are always thinking. Always thinking. Sometimes women cannot even sleep because they will not shut the hell up. While they are lying in bed their mind is just racing about nothing.

Men do the same thing as thoughts run their course in their mind in a racing fashion, overthinking things.

Robert Fritz, in his book *The Path of Least Resistance,* argues that when you think you create. Fritz's compelling logic is that problem-solving leads to reactive oscillation. You go back and forth in our decision making which extends the thinking process.

When we are living in the moment, we must attend to future goal setting and planning. This is a normal process. We just do it with patience and awareness.

Fritz's approach begins with an accurate assessment of the situation at the moment. Then create a vision of where you want to be. This is a key step in manifestation. You become a composer of your life, an artist of living, or a sculptor of bringing out your best features in yourself. You are an architect of your life. You begin to make it happen.

Just let the moment be. When you manifest things naturally, you also begin to shape your behavior.

The reticular activating system is a network of neurons in the brainstem that controls sleep–wake cycles, arousal, and attention. It also helps the brain respond to the environment by triggering fight-or-flight responses. For us as we manifest our future, the reticular activating system opens up stimuli to let things in in which we are interested. It is also meant to block much of the stimuli that you do not care about.

When you focus on something and think about it, signs and signals open up as if the universe is replying to you like a mirror reflecting back to you what you want to manifest.

Living in the moment causes problems that arise in your day-to-day life to become minor speed bumps that you can handle. You use all your knowledge and experience to handle problems that arise with your own direction more than you realize. Do not create a focus of mental anguish that is virtually made up on your mind and is truly not present. You ask yourself, "What is the universe teaching me right now?" You are more resilient than you realize.

Application: Fritz's Thinking Formula

1. Accept what is happening as a current lesson or a situation from which you can learn.
2. In the current moment, make a daily mission and a future vision of what you want. Knowing that when that future appears it will be in that current moment.

3. In the current moment, through your thought process coupled with your vast experience, choose the result that you. This may be an extrapolation of what you have now or something totally new. A bucket list.

4. Stay in the moment, then move on to the next moment without any regard for your future plans. Enjoy your current existence knowing what you want will come to you. The universe will help you naturally manifest it, and it will "flow" in that direction both consciously and unconsciously.

Conclusion

We often search for sages, and we stand on the shoulders of the giants.

As Earl Nightingale states you are sitting on acres of diamonds that are in and of yourself. You are the solution to your own success.

True greatness is in the palm of your hand. The universal power is at your command. You have awesome power to change the moment.

Eckhart Tolle says this perfectly:

Make the current moment your friend and not your enemy. Make the current moment your friend and your whole life will change because the future is just an extension of our current consciousness.

Understanding the brain's fleeting thoughts and the diabolical ego that transpires within us each moment can open up the windows to success. Do not wait too long because the window of success may close on you. Strike while the iron is hot. If you are a student studying, study harder. If you are an executive trying to make your organization greater, strategize better and lead authentically.

Earl Nightingale builds upon this notion of creating your own greatness by saying that you should be planting the right seeds in your brain. The seeds that you plant will grow and be nurtured the same way as the wrong seeds will. Rewire your brain to think positively by planting the correct seeds in your brain, water the seeds and give the seeds sun, and those positive seeds will grow, and you will prosper.

Albert Einstein once said that intelligent people ignore mundane milestones of weakness and focus on their strengths.

If someone yells "stupid" in the streets behind you, you do not turn around to see who it is saying that because you know that they are not referring to you.

When driving, the skid marks you see in front of you indicate problems of the past that missed you; that is why the front windshield is vast and wide. This wide view out of your front window is your vision of your future. Think of the front windshield as encouraging greatness. Then think of your past as the rear-view mirror, in the middle of the car up front and on both sides of the car. These windows provide a rear view in which there are no skid marks that you can see. These views are just past events in your life that do not matter to you anymore.

Keep the focus on your future which is much more important than the things in the rear-view mirror that you leave behind you.

***

CHAPTER 12

Developing the Confidence to Change Your Moment

I listen, I forget.
I see, I remember.
I do, I understand

—Chinese Proverb

Opening Vignette

Tribute to Clay Christensen, a Harvard Business School professor, by Hal Gregersen, on January 30, 2025, on linkedin.com.

When you think of his book *"How to Measure your Life,"* Clay knew, from his own life experience, that little things done well over a long period of time would compound, that it would aggregate into being something beautiful and spectacular.

I think what he was doing, as he maneuvered through life, no matter whom it was with, he was trying to figure out what might the little things be in your world, that if you attended to them better could compound into something powerful, and beautiful, and magnificent.

He had that sense when he worked with organizations, being able to help move companies into that space where they can accomplish great things, but, even more importantly, he was able to help individuals find the space to do amazing things.

It was like he was telling us to think in a certain way. Always asking ourselves, "What might I do here, in this *moment*, that could magnify my life, that could magnify my goodness, that could somehow spark some element of who I am and what I am, to engage more deeply with the world." To ask the most challenging questions you could possibly imagine, of yourself, first, and foremost, and then of others in the world around you, and then do something about it. Because that is just what Clay did over and over and over.

***

Think of how you can develop the confidence to change your moment and be more present and aware of the things you are experiencing with a sense of heightened self-awareness.

Negative feelings could stick with you into adulthood. You must learn to lighten up and have fun in life. Develop a fun-loving personality because the impression you leave on the brain is positive. Being happy helps you live in the moment and not be oblivious to the things around you.

Find joy and compassion within. It is easy to find the faults in life, but it is also easy to find all the good things life brings. Gratitude is key to success in life. Being grateful for the little things helps you navigate the day-to-day stresses life brings.

If you are thinking more outside-in as opposed to inside-out, you will find joy in material things and physical attributes that are tangible. By thinking more inside-out, you begin to have a higher self-worth and self-acceptance because you are intrinsically motivated.

The wisdom of the universe is inside you. Our ego places us in competition with others and keeps us from seeing our true value. This is your past coming back to haunt you. We must free ourselves from the clutches of the past. Do not compare yourself to others.

The wisdom of the universe resides in you. The universe changes and does not remain stagnant and neither do you.

While we are continuously changing, we often try to change people around us. Controlling oneself is hard enough. Attempting to change other people is a waste of your present moment.

We must handle our challenges as they come and not as we wish they would come. Reality is with us every day and attempting to change our reality is fleeting. We adapt, we overcome, and we cannot change what happens to us, but we can change how we react to what happens to us.

Feeling happy for accomplishments when meeting or exceeding your goals and objectives should be celebrated and not shunned upon. When people around you are jealous or envious of your accomplishments, that means that you are doing something right.

The world, in which we live, is meant for people to compare themselves to others, and this comparison could be to your advantage, or it may work against your success in your career or relationships. Stay the course; do not change for other people. Take your life seriously and work hard to accomplish your success.

The key for you is to stay calm, cool, and collected, and use strategic silence when working on a project. Letting the world know what you are doing may cause you to not pursue your dreams because of negative things people say that may prevent you from pursuing your goals, or people deliberately sabotaging your efforts to achieve greatness in life.

Do not let anything bother you and leave the jealousness and envy of others with them. They own the problem. You treat people with kindness and have gratitude and that will spread contagiously.

This will help you stay on course. This will help you to feel the mindsense of abundance as opposed to lack. There is absolutely no reason to worry about the past or be apprehensive of the future.

Mindsense as well as living in the moment is to be exactly who you are without the approval of others. This choice requires you to trust who you are as enough, even though the world may not believe in you and the people around you may judge you according to some standard that may not even exist.

You must be free to express yourself without worrying about other standards and evaluations of yourself. Do not be a different version of yourself to get other people's approval. If your self-worth is tied to the approval of others, then you are not living authentically.

Living authentically is where you are aligned with your true values and beliefs.

The need for perfection is the fear of judgment and fear of failure. By trying to become perfect we limit our potential. It is an attempt to shield us from the vulnerability of being human. By trying to become perfect we miss the purpose of life itself. When you chase perfection, you find yourself in an endless spiral of striving for more.

In this way, you are always unsatisfied because your goals and aspirations are like a moving target that you can never reach. We find ourselves in a spiral of dissatisfaction because we can never get enough.

If you are the type of person in which there is always another flaw to fix, another strategy to pursue, and another goal to achieve, then you may miss the enjoyment of living in the moment.

This endless striving blinds you from the present moment. In your present moment, where your life is happening right now, in all its imperfect glory of perfection, is where you actually are—don't miss it.

You may become so focused on who we think you should be, that you forget to appreciate who you are. But what if, instead of striving for perfection, you embrace imperfection. Imperfection is reality because no one can be perfect all the time. What if you see your flaws not as something that should be hidden or erased but as an essential part of your uniqueness. Just like the imperfect leather jacket that is beautifully messed with cuts and nicks only to be authentic Italian leather. Authentic Italian leather is prized for its exceptional quality, durability, beautiful aging process, and smoothness, which result in a product that lasts for years and becomes more attractive with time. So be like Italian leather and age gracefully.

Your imperfection makes you special; imperfection makes you relatable, and your own imperfection makes you a living human being in a world of artificial intelligence. Artificial intelligence cannot compete with you.

This endless striving for success blinds us to the present moment. Only in the present moment can we engage in what is happening right now and live in life's imperfect glory.

We often become so focused on who we think we should be that we forget to appreciate who we actually are. We must find beauty in the cracks and the chaos.

You are beautiful just as you are and even in the moments that do not go as you planned. When we stop trying to be perfect, we make room for authenticity, we become vulnerable to all possibilities, and we find the freedom to simply be ourselves.

To be alive is to be in a constant state of becoming. By letting go of the illusion of perfection, you allow yourself to flow with life's natural rhythms like a symphony playing perfectly. We begin to see that the beauty of life is not in its flawlessness but in its unpredictability, its spontaneity, and its constant newness. By letting go of the chase for perfection you begin to realize that you are already more than enough.

Comparing yourself to others is probably the worst habit you have developed over your lifetime. It is so easy to find someone smarter, more financially stable, and happier than you are. Do not distort your own perfection. You have your individual fingerprint and that is your uniqueness that makes you special.

Do not judge your accomplishments in comparison to someone else. Realize that you are on your own journey and no two people or people's paths are ever the same. Your journey is shaped by the experiences that you have had, good or bad, and you must live your life loving yourself so that you can find fulfillment. Find value in who you are.

Mindsense as a place of being is feeling truly confident in yourself. A landing zone in which you exist day to day. You place yourself in a parenthesis—in the beginning of the parenthesis, you are born; you live and breathe in the parenthesis; and at the end of the parenthesis, you die.

This logic is limiting but realistic. Live moment to moment.

To be enlightened is to attempt to surround yourself with positive people. Find your strengths and use positive psychology to build on those strengths. This way you give and receive positive energy. Stray away from the negativity, and build on your strengths.

Maslow called it "self-realization." Self-realization is a feeling of enlightenment. No one can get to you. You are in a zone of indifference, and you are feeling alive and aware in the present moment. Self-realization is true enlightenment.

Research in life indicates that the values that you experience in your life shape your behavior. This is compared with your own values, assumptions, beliefs, and expectations. Past consequences cause you to evaluate yourself constantly. This past experience generates feelings and thoughts that corrupt your current moment.

Try using what is called the *rational emotive behavioral model*, which was devised by the psychologist Albert Ellis beginning in the mid-1950s. This model focuses mostly on the present time to help people understand how unhealthy thoughts and beliefs create emotional distress, which, in turn, leads to unhealthy actions and behaviors that interfere with your life and your goals. Through coping strategies like meditation, hypnosis, and relaxation, people tend to view a negative situation, such as a failure or rejection, calmly and rationally.

In order for you to solve your past problems that keep funneling into your mind, think about what you are doing today that is making you think in that way. If you look back at your experiences, you may be bringing them into your present moment for no particular reason other than to relish on past mistakes, mishaps, relationships, goals, objectives, and other things that you perceive as failures. By understanding this thought process, you can say to yourself:

"Ha, here I go again, rehearsing the past again."

Then the simple acknowledgment of the thought diminishes it. This behavior leads to enlightenment.

If you realize that today, in this moment, you are OK, you are happy, and you are content with your life as it is right now, then time is not your enemy any longer. Time, then, is of the essence.

What happened in the past is old news, and a dead issue, that just keeps on recurring in your mind and your thoughts. The only problem that you may have is that you are not living right now in the moment. This moment is all you have.

Your thoughts are taking over your space in the moment. Stop, look, listen, and move on from negative thoughts. After a while, you force yourself to live in the present and forget the things that are holding you back. After doing this often enough, your presence and consciousness begins to be your predominant state and your enlightenment.

Many pop psychologists may ask us to place an X on the thought and say to ourselves, "Stop." This places too much attention on the thought. Just acknowledge the thought and then deflect it so that you are living in the present moment.

This moment, you are truly alive, and your moment-to-moment thinking will recall many aspects of your life, good or bad, but the current moment matters most. Spend each moment with people that matter to you and people that care, and if you are alone, be alone.

Conclusion

By now, you have developed the confidence to change your moment. The key is to look upon yourself as well equipped for any challenge. This moment, you are alive and that is all that matters.

See the beauty in everything and feel good about being alive and having the opportunity to experience life.

When you decide to do something, know what level you're doing it as, novice, beginner, expert, learner, or seasoned expert. No matter what level that you label yourself, do it and do it with your mind, your heart, and your spirit. Whatever you do and the people that you touch will be extraordinary.

***

CHAPTER 13

Living, Loving, and Learning in the Moment

Life is uncharted territory. It reveals its story one moment at a time
—Leo Buscaglia

Living in the moment is now your quest. Loving in the moment is based on how you feel about your relationship status. Learning could be or perhaps should be a continuous process.

These three things, while subtle, can improve your life a great deal. Living your best self, using positive psychology by knowing what your strengths are and honing them will help you to feel enlightened. Loving needs to be a part of you in some way. Love could be with your pet, with your significant other, with your child, or with your grandchild. Learning is the fuel that ignites ambition. Curiosity to learn is the spark to learn and grow and innovation and creativity is the fire inside of you that motivates you to feel great in the moment.

The key is to free yourself from past mistakes and future apprehensions so that you can reap the benefits of your life, and you can enjoy life at its best, right now, right in this moment.

Many people feel that if you had more time in your life that you would spend it with your family and loved ones. Cherish the moments with your loved ones while you can.

Try not to say to yourself I wish I knew then what I know now. Know yourself now.

Temper your cognitive dissonance. Cognitive dissonance is important because it is the state of having inconsistent thoughts, beliefs, or attitudes, especially as related to behavioral decisions and relationships. Develop a routine of self-preservation by tapping these four chemicals in your brain.

- **D**opamine—Your brain needs dopamine for self-reward and for motivation. You find this in exercise, meditation, and new experiences.
- **O**xytocin—Your brain needs this to love people so that you can build a strong connection. You will find this in hugging, socializing, and acts of kindness.
- **S**erotonin—Your brain needs this to keep you in good spirits and in a good mood. You can find this in daily sunshine, giving gratitude, and reveling in the beauty of nature.
- **E**ndorphins—Your brain needs this to diminish both physical and emotional pain and to reduce stress. You find this in exercising to a point where you feel elated.

Joe Dispenza focuses on his basic premise that if you do the same things every day and if you continue to do this, nothing in your life will change. He then provides a simple formula to make change happen.

Joe focuses on thinking your way to a healthy happy lifestyle. His approach is to access your brainwaves for optimal personal healing and better performance on anything that you do in life. Dispenza has helped many people conquer illness.

Joe has many people touting about how he has helped people recover from illness with his methods. His research has led him to develop a practical formula to help people transform their lives.

You may find that Joe Dispenza's research may cause a VABE abrasion in which you feel like there is something you need to do now in the moment to change the way you view the world and the way that you feel the world should be for you.

Vignette—A VABE Abrasion:
The Legendary Kit Carson

In October 1849, a trader named James White, his wife Ann, and their infant daughter were traveling on the Santa Fe Trail to New Mexico when they were attacked by a band of Apache. James was killed, while Ann and the child were taken captive. Major William Grier and a company of Dragoons went in pursuit of the raiders. Their scout was Kit Carson whose sensational, bigger-than-life adventures were being chronicled in popular dime novels of the day. VABES, as discussed, are made up of our values, assumptions, beliefs, and expectations about how you see the world and how the world should be.

On the 12th day out, they spotted a large camp and attacked. As the warriors were fleeing, one fired an arrow into the breast of Mrs. White. Her child was never found.

Mrs. White had been dead only a few minutes and her body was still warm. Among her possessions was a copy of the popular dime novel *Kit Carson: Prince of the Gold Hunters*," a story about Carson saving a beautiful woman from death at the hands of a band of Native Americans. Kit Carson could not read nor write and when the story was read to him, he muttered "Throw it in the fire."

Kit was deeply shaken by the fact that this woman probably died hoping that the famous scout would come to her rescue. Life does not always imitate art. Unlike in the dime novels, Kit Carson got there too late. It was said that the incident haunted Carson for the rest of his life—True West History of the American Frontier

When something goes against your VABES, you have what is called a VABE Abrasion. A VABE abrasion is a temporary feeling that something we thought should be a certain way happens to go against our way of thinking.

In a book by Ed Grant and Cathy Blanche, titled *Kit Carson's Own Story of His Life*, published in 1926, Kit is exploited and faced with a true revelation about himself. Kit lived between December 24, 1809, and May 23, 1868. This story of Kit Carson was published long after his death.

Unfortunately, his attempt to save the woman did not work and Mrs. White died before he could save her. A soldier in the rescue party wrote:

Mrs. White was a frail, delicate, and very beautiful woman, but having undergone such abuse as she suffered while held captive, nothing but a wreck remained; her body was literally covered with blows and scratches. Her countenance even after death indicated a hopeless creature. Over her corpse, we swore vengeance upon her persecutors.

Imagine not only failing to save Mrs. White but seeing a book in her hand with his name on it. A huge VABE Abrasion.

Carson wrote in his Memoirs:

> In camp was found a book, the first of the kind I had ever seen, in which I was made to be a great hero, slaying Native American Indians by the hundreds, and I have often thought that Mrs. White would read the same, and knowing that I lived near, she would pray for my appearance and also pray that she would be saved.

What had happened was that the real Kit Carson had met the fictional Kit Carson, and he was deeply upset at his inability to have saved Mrs. White, for he had failed to live up to the growing myth around himself.

He was sorry for the rest of his life that he had not rescued Mrs. White; the Kit from the dime novel would have saved her. Kit suffered what Jim Clawson, University of Virginia leadership expert, called a "*VABE ABRASION*." Kit had a distinctive feeling that the way the world is and the way the world should be, which have been unimaginably opposite.

Kit Carson (born on December 24, 1809, and died on May 23, 1868) never returned to tracking and never returned to being an expert at knowing the terrain of the Wild West ever again. It has been assumed by many that he was devastated at the picture of Mrs. White's death which was just too much for him to bear.

The lesson here is that you too may have a VABE abrasion and hopefully it is not as devastating as Kit Carson's loss and despair.

***

The famous motivation scholar, known throughout the world, happens to be a man from Brooklyn, New York, by the name of Abraham Maslow.

Maslow felt that the ability to be in the present moment is a major component of mental wellness. Being present, especially in navigating and monitoring the transitions of our thoughts, is enlightenment. Being more present and seeing more deeply translates into being more well centered and more well enlightened.

The present moment could be sabotaged by the four D's of destruction: Doubt, Despair, Detract, Derail, and Despondent.

Thinking destructively is a way of adding too much negativity to your thought process. A slang and unconventional English saying that entails "to get someone's goat" and in this case, get your own goat. The saying came from the French expression *prendre la chevre*, which means to take the goat. The French saying surfaced as one way people could get milk was from a goat, thus, taking the animal would anger its owner.

We often find ourselves delving into our most recent problems while leaving dormant the problems that are more severe in our life. For every problem there is a solution and the solution to your problems is you.

Optimism gives you hope. Hope leads to resilience. Resilience leads to heightened self-awareness. This heightened self-awareness leads to an understanding of the interconnectedness of all things.

When it comes to your thoughts and living in the moment, you are the person that will make your moment the best that it can be, you have a great capacity to change anything that you would like to change in your life.

Diagnose yourself. Ask yourself: ***What do I want from this thought? Is it a memory? A recollection? What do I need right now from this thought? How can I make this thought expand or dissipate?***

Then live in the current moment, which is the only presence that you will ever truly have, right now. Enjoy!

Conclusion

Rewire your brain so that you live, love, and learn in the moment. Come up with three positive things that happened to you during your life. There will always be times in which confusion, fogginess, and conflicting messages may impact your thoughts, and uncertainty may tend to dissipate your energy and ruin your current moment. This is the dance of life and the uncharted future that you are heading into. Life happens not for you but as you. Any negativity is all behind you now. Feel positive and develop your strengths now to be your best self with mindsense.

Mindsense has developed a cadre of ideas orbiting around a core of positive self-regard to be your best-self. This is your time to be present in the moment and prosper in life with your new enlightened self.

You are a confident and an enlightened person now. You mastered mindsense now.

May your day be filled with good thoughts, kind people, and happy moments.

Wherever You Are, Be There in the Moment.

***

Bibliography

Introduction, Preface, and Chapter 1

Anderson, D. 1978. "Nick Fotiu in Wonderland." *New York Times*.

Arbinger Group. 2025. *Leadership and Self-Deception*. ReadHowYouWant Publisher.

Dyer, W. 2005. *The Power of Intention*. Hay House Publications.

Dyer, W. 2009. *Change Your Thoughts—Change Your Life*. Hay House Publications.

Freud, S. 2021. *Psychopathology of Everyday Life*. Fingerprint Publishing.

Hall, B. 2025. *Resolute*. Harper Influence Publications.

Kahneman, D. 2013. *Thinking, Fast and Slow*. Farrar, Straus, and Giroux Publishers.

Kübler-Ross, E. 1997. *Death: The Final Stage of Growth*. Touchstone Book Publishers.

Lally, P., C. H. M. Van Jaarsveld, H. W. W. Potts, and J. Wardle. 2009. "How Are Habits Formed in the Real World." *European Journal of Social Psychology* 40 (6): 998–1009.

Logsdon, J. 2013. *John F. Kennedy and the Race to the Moon*. Palgrave Macmillan.

Maltz, M. 1960. *The New Psycho-Cybernetics*. Prentice Hall.

Maslow, A. H. 2011. *Toward the Psychology of Being*. Wilder Publications.

Nightingale, E. *The Strangest Secret*. Sound Wisdom Publications.

Nightingale, E. 2007. *Think and Grow Rich*. Tarcher Publishing.

Nitoburg, Lev. 1933. "Frog and the Scorpion." *The German Quarter*.

Stone, W. C. 2004. *The Success System That Never Fails*. Executive Book Publishers.

Tichy, N. 2004. *The Cycle of Leadership: How Great Leaders Teach Their Companies to Win*. Harper Business Publications.

Tolle, E. 2004. *The Power of Now: A Guide to Spiritual Enlightenment*. New World Library Publishers.

Watts, A. 1989. *The Book on the Taboo Against Knowing Who You Are*. Vintage Books Publishers.

Chapter 2

Chernow, R. 2018. *Grant*. Penguin Putnam.

Clawson, J. G. 2008. *Level Three Leadership*. Pearson Education.

Clawson, J. G. S., and D. Newberg. 2008. *Powered by Feel: How Individuals, Teams, and Companies Excel*. World Scientific Publishing.

Cross, Rob, and K. Dillon. 2023 "The Hidden Toll of Microstress: Small, Difficult Moments Can Zap Your Performance. Here's How to Restore Your Well-Being." *Harvard Business Review*, February 7.

Cross, R., J. Dillon, and H. Martin. 2024. "5 Ways to Deal with the Microstresses Draining Your Energy." *Harvard Business Review*, February 29.

Csikszentmihalyi, Mihaly. *Flow: The Psychology of Optimal Experience*. New York: Harper & Row, 2009.

Csikszentmihalyi, Mihaly. *Flow and the Foundations of Positive Psychology: The Collected Works of Mihaly Csikszentmihalyi*. Dordrecht: Springer, 2016.

Curtis, S. 1998. *Zorro Unmasked: The Official History*. Hyperion Publishers.

Daniels, P. 1985. *How to Reach Your Life Goals*. The House of Tabor Publishers.

Disney, R. H. 2004. *The Three Little Pig*. Random House Publishers.

Goddard, N. 2016. *Out of This World: Reshape Your Future by Using Your Imagination*. CreateSpace Independent Publishing.

Grodin, Charles, and Robert De Niro. actors. 1988. *Midnight Run Film*. Image Entertainment.

Hoffer, Eric. *Public Figure: The American Philosopher, Eric Hoffer (1902–1983)*. "Eric Hoffer, Genius—And Enigma." Hoover Institution.

Lee, B. 1998. *Bruce Lee the Art of Expressing the Human Body*. Tuttle Publishing.

Maltz, M. 1960. *The New Psycho-Cybernetics*. Prentice Hall.

Peters, L. 1998. *The Peter Principle: Why Things Always Go Wrong*. Harper Perennial Publishers.

Welch, E. 2011. *What Do You Think of Me: Why Do I Care*. New Growth Press.

Chapter 3

Cole-Whittaker, T. 2020. *What You Think of Me Is None of My Business*. Penguin Putnam Publishers. Byrne, Rhonda. *The Secret*. New York: Simon & Schuster, 2011.

Donahue, E. M. And Kentle, R. L. (1991): *Big Five Inventory (BFI)*. APA Psycological Tests.

Frankl, V. 2006. *Man's Search for Meaning*. Beacon Press.

Goldberg, L. 1936. "The 'Big Five Personality Traits Model.' " In *Everything Psychology Book*, edited by Kendra Cherry.

Gove, B. 2025. *Father of Professional Speaking*.

Jacks, L. P. 1934. *The Revolt Against Mechanism*. Golden Rare Books.

JFK Library. "John F. Kennedy Quotations." *John F. Kennedy Presidential Library and Museum*. Accessed May 15, 2025. https://www.jfklibrary.org.

Mintzberg, H., and J. Gosling. 2003. "The Five Minds of a Manager." *Harvard Business Review*, November.

Mother Goose's. *Nursery Rhymes*. Humpty Dumpty, introduced in Mother Goose's Nursery Rhymes in which most children first heard the rhyme. The story of

Humpty Dumpty is based on a cannon used by the Royalists during the English Civil War. The cannon was positioned on the walls of Colchester. When the Parliamentary forces damaged the walls, the cannon fell to the ground.

Nightingale, E. *The Strangest Secret*. Sound Wisdom Publications.

Pritchett, P. 2006. *The Quantum Leap Strategy*. Pritchett LP Publisher.

RadioX. 2025. "The Heartbreaking True Story Behind the Beatles' Song *LET IT BE, Found on radiox.co.uk.*"

McGreal, Sister Nona, OP. "A Brief History of the Dominican Order in the U.S." *Dominican University*. Accessed May 15, 2025. https://www.dom.edu/your-link-here.

Schulz, C. M. 2024. *Peanuts: The Second Classic Peanuts Collection*. Titan Comics Publishers.

Waitley, D. 1984. *The Psychology of Winning: Ten Qualities of a Total Winner*. Berkley Publishing.

Wattles, W. 2007. *The Science of Getting Rich*. Tarcher/Penguin Publisher.

Chapter 4

Allen, J. (1902) 2021. *As a Man Thinketh*. Independently Published.

Clawson, J. G. 2008. *Level Three Leadership*. Pearson Education.

Covey, S. 2025. *Seven Habits of Highly Effective People*. Franklin Covey Publisher.

Doty, J. 2025. "The Universe Doesn't Give a F*ck About You!" YouTube video.

Goddard, N. 2015. *The Power of Imagination*. Tarcher Publisher.

Kahneman, D. 2013. *Thinking, Fast and Slow*. Farrar, Straus, and Giroux Publishers.

Marshall, Garry. director. 1990. *Pretty Woman Film*. adapted from the Pygmalion.

Meshram, R. 2018. "How Common Is It for People to Never Be in a Romantic Relationship?" Quora.com.

Nightingale, E. 2007. *Think and Grow Rich*. Tarcher Publishing.

Owen, J. P. 2015. *Cowboy Ethics: What It Takes to Win at Life*. Skyhouse Publishers.

Provitera, M. J. 2012. *Mastering Self-Motivation*. Business Expert Press.

Sincero, J. 2006. *You Are a Badass: How to Stop Doubting Your Greatness and Start Living an Awesome Life*. John Murray Learning Publishers.

Thoreau, H. D. 2024. *Walden*. This Nielsen UK Publishers.

Tiger Lily. "The Flower That Dares You to Be Fearless." *Petal Republic*. Accessed May 15, 2025.

Chapter 5

Crossley, H. 2009. *The Golden Sayings of Epictetus*. Ezreads Publications.

Langer, E. J. 2014. *Mindfulness*. Harvard Publishers.

Nightingale, Earl J. *The Strangest Secret*. Stanford, CA: Stanfordpub.com, 2017. Paperback.

Reagan, N. 2022. "The 'Just Say No to Drugs' Campaign."
Watts, A. 1989. *The Book on the Taboo Against Knowing Who You Are*. Vintage Books Publishers.

Chapter 6

Dyer, W. 2009. *Change Your Thoughts—Change Your Life*. Hay House Publications.
Hunter, Sam, writer. 2022. *The Whale*.
Nightingale, E. *The Strangest Secret*. Sound Wisdom Publications, 2017.
Rulkens, Paul. *The Michelangelo Principle*. 2024
Rulkens, P. 2024. *The Michelangelo Principle*. Business Expert Press.
Watts, A. 1989. *The Book on the Taboo Against Knowing Who You Are*. Vintage Books Publishers.
William James. *Encyclopedia Britannica*. Accessed May 15, 2025.

Chapter 7

Dyer, W. 2005. *The Power of Intention*. Hay House Publications.
Franklin, B. *The Autobiography of Benjamin Franklin: A Benjamin Franklin Autobiography Classics*. Warbler Classics, 2022. Originally published 1791.
Isaacson, W. 2021. *Albert Einstein: The Man, the Genius, and the Theory of Relativity*. Rosen Young Adult Publishers.
Jung, C. G. 2003. *Psychology of the Unconscious*. Dover Publications.
Wattles, W. 2007. *The Science of Getting Rich*. Tarcher/Penguin Publisher.
Genius Wave, found on website called forgeniuswave.com with a link Genius Wave.

Chapter 8

Abrashoff, D. M. 2012. *It's Your Ship: Management Techniques from the Best Damn Ship in the Navy*. Grand Central Publishing.
Cox, Valerie. "The Cookie Thief." Public Domain, 2017.

Chapter 9

Armstrong, Thomas. 2020. "The Stages of Life According to Carg Jung." *American Institute for Learning and Human Development*. Accessed June 16, 2025. https://www.institute4learning.com/2020/04/10/the-stages-of-life-according-to-carl-jung/
Csikszentmihalyi, M. 1991. *Flow: They Psychology of Optimal Experience*. Harper Perennial Publishers.

Dyer, W. 2005. *The Power of Intention*. Hay House Publications.

Roberts, L. M., E. Heaphy, and B. B. Caza. 2019. "To Become Your Best Self, Study Your Successes." *Harvard Business Review*, May 14.

Roberts, L. M., G. M. Spreitzer, J. E. Dutton, R. E. Quinn, E. Heaphy, and B. B. Caza. 2005. "How to Play to Your Strengths." *Harvard Business Review*, January.

Sim Sitkin, a Duke's Fuqua School of Business professor or leadership, said, at an Academy of Management.

Sitkin, Sim. 2025. "Personal Conference Session on Leadership." Paper Presented at the 85th Annual Meeting of the Academy of Management, Copenhagen, Denmark, July 25–29, 2025. Cambridge University Press.

Sitkin, Sim B., Laura B. Cardinal, and Katinka Bijlsma-Frankema. 2010. "Organizational Control." In *Cambridge Companions to Management*. Cambridge University Press.

Chapter 10

Cassata, M. A. 2010. *Essential Jim Carrey: An Unofficial Fan Guide*. BearManor Media Publishers.

Csikszentmihalyi, M. 1991. *Flow: They Psychology of Optimal Experience*. Harper Perennial Publishers.

Dispenza, J. 2008. *Evolve Your Brain: The Science of Changing Your Mind*. Health Communications.

Doty, J. R. 2024. *Mind Magic: The Neuroscience of Manifestation and How It Changes Everything*. Avery Publishers.

John, E. 2019. *Me: Elton John Official Autobiography*. Henry Holt.

Stallone, S. 2005. *Sly Moves: My Proven Program to Lose Weight, Build Strength, Gain Will Power, and Live Your Dream*. William Morrow Publishers.

Taraborrelli, J. R. 2009. *The Secret Life of Marilyn Monroe*. Grand Central Publishing.

Zig Ziglar. n.d. "Zig Ziglar on Leadership." Performed by: Zig Ziglar, Tom Ziglar, Length: 3 hrs 13 mins. https://www.audible.com/mk/t/title-3?asin=B0 18Y8HH7I&source_code=GO1PP30DTRIAL54703142491H0&gad_ source=1&gad_campaignid=16881025087&gclid=CjwKCAjwgb_ CBhBMEiwA0p3oOMExjE1iJjJGLhpbwXiLveW5F4K4Wjdba 0NMVStZ0PnEbE_OAB6MQhoCCXAQAvD_BwE&gclsrc=aw.ds

Chapter 11

Fritz, R. 1989. in his book *The Path of Least Resistance: Learning to Become the Creative Force in Your Life*. Ballantine Books Publisher.

Isaacson, Walter. 2018. *Albert Einstein: The Man, the Genius, and the Theory of Relativity*. Wellbeck Publishing Group Limited. Great Thinkers Series.

Nightingale, E. 2007. *Think and Grow Rich*. Tarcher Publishing.

Sykes, Wanda. 2025. "Ladies, Remember the Last Time Your Brain Had a Moment of Silence?" June 16, 2025. https://www.youtube.com/shorts/V91Zl4R7c5Y

Tolle, E. 2004. *The Power of Now: A Guide to Spiritual Enlightenment*. New World Library Publishers.

Chapter 12

Christensen, C. M. 2003. *The Innovator's Dilemma: The Revolutionary Book That Will Change the Way You Do Business*. Collins Business Essentials Publishers.

Maslow, A. H. 2011. *Toward the Psychology of Being*. Wilder Publications.

Chapter 13

Clawson, J. G. 2008. *Level Three Leadership*. Pearson Education.

Dispenza, J. 2008. *Evolve Your Brain: The Science of Changing Your Mind*. Health Communications.

Grant, E., and C. Blanche. 1926. *Kit Carson's Own Story of His Life*. Kit Carson Memorial Foundation.

Maslow, A. H. 2011. *Toward the Psychology of Being*. Wilder Publications.

About the Author

Dr. Michael J. Provitera is Associate Professor of Management and Certified Positive Psychology Coach and Facilitator. Mike is an editor with Business Expert Press for the Organizational Behavior and Human Resource Management Collection.

His focus is on improving organizational effectiveness and enhancing individual success. He has trained over 1,000 executives and taught management to over 2,000 undergraduate and graduate students.

Clients of his have been Pfizer, Trane, CEO Business, Interval International, Global Conference Alliance Inc., City of Sunrise Fire Rescue, and the City of North Miami.

Michael is sought by reporters for quotations in prominent media such as *Forbes*, U.S. News & World Report, *The Daily News*, Fox Business, Higher Ed Jobs, HR.com, NBC News, and *The Washington Times*.

Index

Mintzberg, Henry, 37
Moment, the, 85–93
  being present in, 65–73
  confidence to change, 125–131
  of conscientiousness, 51–64
  emotional moments of resonance,
    17–32
  of Enlightenment, 95–102
  give in to, 111–117
  of going with the flow, 103–109
  learning, 133–138
  living in, 112, 133–138
  loving in, 133–138
  power to change, 119–124
  in ship's wake, 33–49
  trust and faith in, 111
  in the universe, 75–84
Money, 112

N
Naptime in kindergarten, 52
Negative feelings, 126
Negative thoughts, 112
Negativeness, 108
Negativity, 44
Neuroplasticity, 9, 12
Neuroticism, 43
Newberg, Doug, 18
Nightingale, Earl, 12, 35, 57, 67, 75,
    84, 119–120, 123

O
Openness, 42
Optimism, 47, 49
Overthinking, 120, 121
Oxytocin, 134

P
Pandora method, 65
The Path of Least Resistance (Fritz),
    122
Peace of mind, 3, 10, 15, 32, 34, 57,
    70, 117
Perfection, 127–128
Personal leadership, 109
Peters, Laurence, 23
Poker face, 82, 83
Pomodoro technique, 65

Positive psychology, 19
The Power of Intention (Dyer), 13
Power to change the moment,
    119–124
Pretty Woman (movie), 63
Provitera, Ann, 70
Provitera, Michael, 55
Psycho-cybernetics, 31
Psychological fear, 25

Q
Quantum physics, 13

R
Rational emotive behavioral model,
    129
Reagan, Nancy, 68
Relaxation, 52, 68, 85–87, 130
Repetition, 113
Resilience, 4, 47, 49, 137
Resolute (Hall), 4
Resonance, 79, 85
  emotional moments of, 17–32
Reticular activating system, 122
Rohn, Jim, 33, 111
Romeo and Juliet, 62
Roosevelt, Franklin D., 17, 24

S
Schulz, Charles M., 34
The Secret (film), 35
Self-acceptance, 126
Self-awareness, 37, 61, 66, 104, 113,
    121, 137
Self-concept, 25
Self-criticism, 55
Self-discipline, 66
Self-efficacy, 80
Self-esteem, 25, 80, 113
Self-knowledge, 20, 37
Self-leadership, 30, 32, 37
Self-preservation, 25, 133
Self-realization, 129
Self-talk, 1
Self-worth, 126, 127
Semiconsciousness behavior, 60
Serotonin, 134
Shakespeare, 62, 99